BFI Film Classics

The BFI Film Classics is a series of books that introduces, interprets and celebrates landmarks of world cinema. Each volume offers an argument for the film's 'classic' status, together with discussion of its production and reception history, its place within a genre or national cinema, an account of its technical and aesthetic importance, and in many cases, the author's personal response to the film.

For a full list of titles available in the series, please visit our website: <www.palgrave.com/bfi>

'Magnificently concentrated examples of flowing freeform critical poetry.'
Uncut

'A formidable body of work collectively generating some fascinating insights into the evolution of cinema.'
Times Higher Education Supplement

'The series is a landmark in film criticism.'
Quarterly Review of Film and Video

D1713806

Back to the Future

Andrew Shail &
Robin Stoate

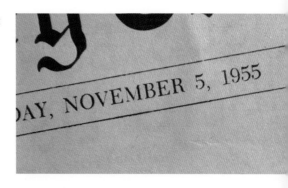

DAY, NOVEMBER 5, 1955

palgrave
macmillan

A BFI book published by Palgrave Macmillan

First published in 2010 by
PALGRAVE MACMILLAN

on behalf of the

BRITISH FILM INSTITUTE
21 Stephen Street, London W1T 1LN
www.bfi.org.uk

There's more to discover about film and television through the BFI. Our world-renowned archive, cinemas, festivals, films, publications and learning resources are here to inspire you.

PALGRAVE MACMILLAN in the UK is an imprint of Macmillan Publishers Limited, registered in England, company number 785998, of Houndmills, Basingstoke, Hampshire RG21 6XS. Palgrave Macmillan in the US is a division of St Martin's Press LLC, 175 Fifth Avenue, New York, NY 10010. Palgrave Macmillan is the global academic imprint of the above companies and has companies and representatives throughout the world. Palgrave® and Macmillan® are registered trademarks in the United States, the United Kingdom, Europe and other countries.

Series cover design: Ashley Western
Series text design: ketchup/SE14
Images from *Back to the Future*, © Universal City Studios, Inc.; p. 15 – *Star Wars*, Lucasfilm Ltd/20th Century-Fox Film Corporation; p. 103 – *Family Guy*, 20th Century-Fox Television; pp. 105–6 – *Indiana Jones and the Kingdom of the Crystal Skull*, © Lucasfilm Ltd.

Printed in China

This book is printed on paper suitable for recycling and made from fully managed and sustained forest sources. Logging, pulping and manufacturing processes are expected to conform to the environmental regulations of the country of origin.

British Library Cataloguing-in-Publication Data
A catalogue record for this book is available from the British Library

ISBN 978–1–84457–293–9

Contents

Introduction

Zemeckis, Gale ...

Released in the USA on 3 July 1985, *Back to the Future* was the year's runaway summer blockbuster. Boosted by heavy radio rotation of Huey Lewis and the News' 'The Power of Love' in the weeks before release, it faced down *Rambo*, *Cocoon*, *Brewster's Millions*, *Mad Max: Beyond Thunderdome* and *A View to a Kill* to become the top-grossing film of 1985 and the eighth highest-grossing film of the 1980s. Co-written by Robert Zemeckis and his long-time collaborator Bob Gale, and directed by Zemeckis, it was the first significant foray into the visibly effects-laden film-making for which the director has since become famous. Later examples include *Who Framed Roger Rabbit?* (1988), two *Back to the Future* sequels (1989 and 1990), *Death Becomes Her* (1992), *Forrest Gump* (1994), *Contact* (1997), *The Polar Express* (2004) and *Beowulf* (2007), although visual effects feature heavily in such 'non-effects' films as *Cast Away* (2000). Zemeckis was a prominent, albeit slightly younger, member of a generation of film-makers centred on Steven Spielberg and George Lucas, and one of the major directors of Hollywood's reformed product of the post-1975 era. His early career was extensively shaped by contact with Spielberg and another of the more established members of this generation, screenwriter/director John Milius (director of, among others, *Big Wednesday* [1978], *Conan the Barbarian* [1982] and *Red Dawn* [1984]).

After extensive work on home-made 8mm films during his childhood in south Chicago, Zemeckis was accepted by the School of Cinematic Arts at the University of Southern California on the strength of one of these films; the School had also produced Lucas and Milius, and it was here that Zemeckis first met Gale. Graduating in 1973, with the USC Academy Award for Best Film for his final-year project, *Field of Honor*, in hand, he brokered a meeting with Spielberg and Milius to show them the film. Zemeckis and Gale built up a friendship with Spielberg and Milius, and while clamouring for scriptwriting work for the Los Angeles-based television companies, they called on Spielberg's help in getting Sid Sheinberg (then president of Universal parent company MCA and keen Spielberg advocate) to agree to finance their co-written *I Wanna Hold Your Hand* (April 1978), with Zemeckis directing, on the condition that Spielberg act as executive producer. Zemeckis's second commercial film, *Used Cars* (July 1980), again featured Gale as co-writer and Spielberg as executive producer (this time along with Milius). Both films fared poorly, however, with *I Wanna Hold Your Hand* costing $2.7 million to produce and grossing only $1.94 million over its lifetime, while *Used Cars* cost $8 million to produce and grossed only $11.7 million over its lifetime. Zemeckis and Gale also collaborated with Milius on the script for Spielberg's *1941* (1979), but this project likewise performed poorly, costing $35 million to produce and achieving a domestic gross of just $31.76 million over its lifetime. It is one of only three of Spielberg's twenty-four cinema releases to date to realise a lifetime domestic gross lower than its production budget (the others were *A.I.* [2001] and *Munich* [2005]), although the gross from foreign markets has enabled all three to exceed their production costs.

Following the release of *Used Cars*, Bob Gale visited his parents in St Louis, Missouri, where, upon finding his father's high-school yearbook, he came up with the concept for a film about meeting one's parents when they were one's own age. He and Zemeckis then approached Columbia, who, in September 1980, gave them a development deal for a film about a time-travelling teenager. When they saw the first script for *Back to the Future* in February 1981, however, Columbia put the film in 'turnaround' (i.e. they were willing to sell it to another studio for the price of development so far), and Zemeckis resolved not to accept Spielberg's subsequent offer to produce it. Following his earlier financial failures, Zemeckis was both reluctant to damage Spielberg's reputation further and unwilling to cultivate a reputation as a director/writer whose work was so poor that it was only made in the first place because it was championed by the industrially influential Spielberg. Instead, Zemeckis and Gale immediately revised the script again, but over the following three years it was rejected roughly forty times by the major studios and production companies, most of whom saw it as insufficiently salacious to function as a contemporary teenpic (although Disney rejected it as too risqué).[1] But in 1983, Michael Douglas (a fan of *Used Cars*), who was set to produce and star in *Romancing the Stone*, convinced 20th Century-Fox to invite Zemeckis to direct. The film was released in March 1984, and following its box-office success (produced for $11.14 million, it grossed $69.57 million in its first sixteen weeks, and became the eighth highest-grossing film of 1984), Universal picked up *Back to the Future*. Zemeckis, who was now, in his view, free of the stigma of being unable to work without Spielberg's help, accepted it. This included the services of Spielberg's production company, Amblin (founded by Spielberg, Kathleen Kennedy and Frank Marshall in 1984, and based in the Universal complex). During October 1984, Spielberg worked with Zemeckis and Gale on making further revisions to the script. Principal photography ran from November 1984 to April 1985 (including an abortive start with Eric Stoltz as Marty McFly). After a very successful test screening in May, the film was rushed through the final stages of post-production, including scoring and sound mixing, to be ready for release on Wednesday 3 July, just before the key calendar spot of the Fourth of July weekend. Produced for roughly $19 million, it achieved a domestic gross of $18.48 million in its first seven days, $36.43 million in its first fortnight, $140.1 million after ten weeks and $190.58 million by the end of the year, eventually earning Universal $94 million in revenue. As the film was written, produced and distributed as a stand-alone unit (the 'To be continued ...' after the final shot was only added to the video version released the following year), we will restrict our analysis to the 1985 film.

... and Hollywood's Revivalists

In September 1978, David Colker and Jack Virrel proposed that
America was witnessing the rise of what they proposed to call
'New New Hollywood'.[2] While the term 'New Hollywood' has
been used to refer to an American 'New Wave' phase of film-making
lasting from roughly 1967 to 1976, which included such films as
Bonnie and Clyde (dir. Arthur Penn, 1967), *Easy Rider* (dir. Dennis
Hopper, 1969), *Midnight Cowboy* (dir. John Schlesinger, 1969),
Five Easy Pieces (dir. Bob Rafelson, 1970), *The Conversation*
(dir. Francis Ford Coppola, 1974), *The Parallax View* (dir. Alan
Pakula, 1974), *Chinatown* (dir. Roman Polanski, 1974) and *Taxi
Driver* (dir. Martin Scorsese, 1976),[3] it is also used to refer to a later
phase of film-making that began in the mid-to-late 1970s and
centred on the contemporaries and protégés of Spielberg. The first
major landmarks of this second 'New Hollywood' (still arguably
ongoing) included *Jaws* (dir. Steven Spielberg, 1975), *Star Wars* (dir.
George Lucas, 1977), its sequels in 1980 (dir. Irvin Kershner) and
1983 (dir. Richard Marquand), *Superman* (dir. Richard Donner,
1978), *Raiders of the Lost Ark* (dir. Steven Spielberg, 1981),
its sequels in 1984 and 1989, *E.T.* (dir. Steven Spielberg, 1982),
Gremlins (dir. Joe Dante, 1984), *Ghostbusters* (dir. Ivan Reitman,
1984) and *Back to the Future*. Even in 1978, Colker and Virrel had
cited Zemeckis and Gale as examples of the latter. We will follow
them and, more recently, Jon Lewis, Thomas Elsaesser and David
Bordwell, among others, in distinguishing it as 'New New
Hollywood'.[4]

　　'New Hollywood' has been viewed by some as a brief window
of openness to film production that drew on the influence of
European art cinema, with 'New New Hollywood' heralding a
recanting of such experimentation. But although not all film
historians distinguish between these two phases with reference to film
form (many simply regard *Jaws* as heralding a later permutation of
the same post-classical film type), they are more united in identifying
Jaws as the herald of a break from New Hollywood's funding and

marketing practices.[5] Just as with the French *nouvelle vague* films of 1959 to *c.*1968 on which they drew, the major New Hollywood successes of the late 1960s and early 1970s attracted funding because they seemed to offer the industry a solution to the problems of rapidly declining cinema attendances and apparently failing traditional film-making formulae. Another result of this decline was that by the mid-1970s, most of the major Hollywood studios, which were all now essentially financing and distribution companies, were in the hands of large multi-industry concerns, most of which had no previous holdings in entertainments. In spite of the capacity of these companies to compensate for the drain of a loss-making film-financing arm, their executives nonetheless treated the studios as they would their other holdings: the huge financial investments required for the production of each film were to realise correspondingly massive returns with little probability of loss. Hollywood had converted to funding films as single units shortly after the break-up of the studio system in the late 1940s, with the result that loss-making films were no longer systemically normal, but the rise of this new ownership meant that the pressure to build films from assured profit-making components increased significantly.

One consequence of this was the resurgence of the blockbuster, as production values were leaned on to ensure profitability. Whereas blockbusters or equivalents had comprised an occasional part of Hollywood's mode of operation since the emergence of the feature film immediately before the First World War, and had even become an area of particular speculation following the break-up of the studio system, the box-office failure of such lavish blockbusters as 20th Century-Fox's *Doctor Dolittle* (dir. Richard Fleischer, 1967), *Star!* (dir. Robert Wise, 1968) and *Hello Dolly* (dir. Gene Kelly, 1969) was one motive for the openness to formal experimentation and counter-culture alienation that enabled the rise of New Hollywood, which produced A-class features rather than blockbusters.[6] New New Hollywood saw the industry not only return to the blockbuster but commence funding it as its primary product.[7] These films were also now expected to realise their potential for profit in the opening few weeks, before flaws in the film might damage its reputation, with the result that saturation release patterns and intensive advance advertising or 'front-loading' became common practice.

Jaws received a promotional budget of $2.5 million (its production budget was only $7 million) for an opening on 20 June 1975, was the first big-budget film to be marketed through saturation advertising on television, and the first to open simultaneously as widely as possible (at 409 cinemas) rather than in the existing system of radiating run zones. Just as New Hollywood represented an attempt to solve the problem of declining audiences by producing films aimed at the more specific 'youth' audience (and thus risking offending others), the New New Hollywood blockbuster was the attempt of the conglomerate parent business to construct a customer base that was as close to universal as possible.

    Back to the Future was treated to this blockbuster status. Composer Alan Silvestri was instructed to produce a score appropriate for a film of epic scale, and used the largest orchestra to perform for a Universal film so far.[8] In the absence of the newly essential formula component of a recently published novel (tying in the film with Peter Benchley's recently published *Jaws* [1974] had been fundamental to the huge success of Spielberg's *Jaws*), the tie-in with Huey Lewis and the News, one of the most popular contemporary bands, was viewed as crucial. In addition, on approving the project, Sheinberg asked that *Back to the Future* be ready for Memorial Day weekend (25–27 May), the major holiday weekend that has since come to mark the start of the summer film season; although this deadline wasn't met, the film's eventual opening on the Fourth of July weekend was just as significant, as these long weekends provide the optimum conditions for potential customers to become actual cinemagoers, ensuring that films released on these dates are able to realise as much of the film's box-office potential as possible, and quickly. *Back to the Future* opened simultaneously at 1,340 cinemas, a number that increased steadily to a peak of 1,550 cinemas in its ninth week, roughly a fifth of all US cinemas at the time.[9] The numerous rejections of their earlier versions of *Back to the Future* also hint that Zemeckis and Gale were working on a blockbuster from the start, as they unwittingly tried to pitch as a specialist teenpic a film with the much wider audience appeal of the post-*Jaws* era.

Zemeckis and Gale also fall into the New New Hollywood camp by virtue of being members of the first generation of Americans to have had no experience of life before television. Zemeckis recalls that during his upbringing in Chicago in the 1950s and 1960s, his only cultural activity was watching television.[10] Television thus provided a substantial portion of the film's cultural reference points, from *The Honeymooners* (the 1955–6 show starring Jackie Gleason that Marty calls a classic and that he apes in imitating an alien) to *Star Trek* (1966–9). The experience of watching television also meant that a concatenated experience of film history via television syndications of the studios' back catalogues was a major aspect of their upbringing.[11] This led both to their affection for classical Hollywood and a tendency to regard cinema and television as possessing equal cultural status, which made television a relevant source of content and stylistic basis for cinema. Zemeckis noted that when he and Gale were writing the script, they imagined Marty and Doc's relationship as equivalent to that between the initially seven-year-old Theodore 'Beaver' Cleaver and his elderly (and only true) friend Gus the retired fireman, protagonists in the situation comedy *Leave It to Beaver* (1957–63).[12] Vivian Sobchack also regards television as a major influence. For her, the film's *mise en scène* 'spatializes neither 1955 nor 1985, but the television time of "Leave It to Beaver" and "Father Knows Best" [1954–60]. Marty's home town thus has only a pseudo-historical existence, as an earlier representation in a previous *text*.'[13] She sees the small towns and suburban neighbourhoods of 1950s television as providing the foundations for most of the films of Spielberg and his protégés.

New New Hollywood products are frequently perceived as aesthetically deficient in comparison with those of the 1967–76 'wave'. Zemeckis and Gale's writing process even backs this up. They would generate set pieces and then produce the corresponding scenes necessary for these set pieces to work. For example, if Marty was to stand in for the wounded guitarist at the dance, it would be essential to establish beforehand that he could play the guitar, which necessitated the earlier audition scene.[14] (Most of these set pieces were related to conveying the single motif of Marty's incongruity in the 1950s.) Dialogue and action follow only thereafter. Notably, a varying relationship to narrative cinema is suggested by the fact that Zemeckis's first commercial success – *Romancing the Stone* – was the first film he had directed that he had not also written. New New Hollywood directors have nonetheless treated this generational schism as positive, Zemeckis and Gale claiming that they gravitated towards each other at USC because they both elected to ignore older students', and New Hollywood's, preoccupation with the French *nouvelle vague* in favour of classical Hollywood directors:

[t]he graduate students at USC had this veneer of intellectualism, and the undergraduates didn't have that yet, or ever. So Bob [Gale] and I gravitated toward one another because we wanted to make Hollywood movies. We weren't interested in the French New Wave. We were interested in Clint Eastwood and James Bond and Walt Disney, because that's how we grew up.[15]

Zemeckis and Gale also attended USC at a time when auteurism was the reigning form of film scholarship at universities. This French-led school of thought (broadcast in America by *Village Voice* columnist Andrew Sarris during the 1960s) held that in spite of the collaborative nature of film, directors were equivalent to painters rather than orchestral conductors in that their own individuality would, even unconsciously, imprint itself on each of their films, leaving an identifiable signature coded in such elements as camera movement, composition, shot duration, editing structures and uses of colour and sound. But auteur criticism did not focus on French directors. As it had its origins in post-occupation France, when a

backlog of five years of American films had been released in a highly
compressed period, this regard for certain directors as auteurs tended
to concentrate on 1940s classical Hollywood directors such as
Howard Hawks, John Ford and Alfred Hitchcock.[16] Zemeckis cites
just such classic American directors, particularly Billy Wilder and
Frank Capra, as the major influences on *Back to the Future*,[17] overtly
reached back to early classical Hollywood in the allusion (in the
climactic scene) to Harold Lloyd, as 'The Boy', hanging from a clock
on the side of a building in *Safety Last!* (dirs. Fred C. Newmeyer &
Sam Taylor, 1923) and, in a clear signal of the equal relevance for his
generation of film and television, described the film as a cross
between Capra and *The Twilight Zone* (1959–64).[18]

Even though New Hollywood is traditionally seen as America's
open encounter with the influence of auteurism, and New New
Hollywood as the industry's alternative to film-making that wore its
director's idiolect on its sleeve, auteurism was not incompatible with
industrially determined production. Its original French proponents
had argued that even (and especially) the most restricted production-
line studio-era directors had impressed their films with implicit
signatures. Although the issue of whether a film's director can be
treated as the sole originating consciousness of a film becomes less
fraught when that director was also a co-writer, this doubling-up is
itself an expression of directors' own convictions that cinema, rather
than being innately collaborative, can be a matter of sole (or dual)
authorship.

If New New Hollywood is often known as the 'Spielberg–Lucas
generation', the primacy of these names is not unwarranted.
Amblin's activities meant that Spielberg served as either producer or
executive producer on nineteen films during its first six years, and
although Zemeckis is Spielberg's most successful protégé, through
Amblin, Spielberg also helped to launch the careers of Joe Dante,
Lawrence Kasdan, Don Bluth and Simon Wells, and produced for
such established directors as Akira Kurosawa, Martin Scorsese and
Clint Eastwood. Lucas's Industrial Light and Magic, founded in 1975

to pick up the work of 20th Century-Fox's recently closed effects department, worked on the film's thirty-two effects shots (including point-of-view shots through the windscreen of the car when Marty travels back in time, which closely resemble Luke Skywalker's view through the screen of his X-Wing), and this relationship played a substantial part in converting Zemeckis to an effects-heavy director. As Stephen Prince points out, it was via these collaborations that 'a massive number of films in the period [i.e. the 1980s] exemplified what might be called the Spielberg–Lucas style'.[19] Of the fourteen top-grossing films (adjusted for inflation) of the period from 1977 to 1986, in which *Back to the Future* ranks ninth, half, including the top five, involved either Spielberg or Lucas, or both.[20]

Industrial Light and Magic stays true to form

An established auteur when he founded Amblin, Spielberg, in particular, made it his job to sponsor the idea of auteurism.[21] He even took a direct hand in defending Zemeckis and Gale's authorial integrity with *Back to the Future*. When, having agreed to finance production, Sheinberg sent a memo to the major figures requiring a title change to *Spaceman from Pluto* and outlining the corresponding script alterations, Spielberg came to Zemeckis and Gale's aid by replying with his thanks for the hilarious joke memo.[22] Although this story pokes fun at the unknowing studio executive, the studios made much of directorial authorship as a way of pre-selling films. As Timothy Corrigan argues, in the 1980s, after the waning of the heavily directorial American 'New Wave', the director 'rematerialised … as an agent of a commercial performance of the business of being an auteur'.[23] Advertising for *Back to the Future*, for example, made overt assertions of Zemeckis's authorship. Posters for *I Wanna Hold Your Hand* had listed no one immediately above or below the title, while those for both *Used Cars* and *Romancing the Stone* featured just the names of the recognisable stars. However, the iconic posters featuring Marty staring disbelievingly at his watch were headed 'Steven Spielberg presents *Back to the Future*, a Robert Zemeckis film'. This layout was repeated for the two sequels, and on publicity for most of his films since, 'A Robert Zemeckis film' has appeared above the title. As Chapter 1 will show, Zemeckis's part in this new generation is borne out in *Back to the Future*'s cinematography and its treatment of genre.

1 'You're gonna see some serious shit': New New Hollywood in Action

Form and style

If Stephen Prince's 'Spielberg–Lucas style' was the light-hearted and comedic presentation of action-heavy and spectacle-oriented adventure melodrama, then *Back to the Future* clearly signals Zemeckis's participation in this. As Peter Krämer notes, Zemeckis has told

intimate stories, either about childlike men (Marty McFly, Roger Rabbit, Forrest Gump, even to some extent Chuck Noland in *Cast Away*) and their familial or quasi-familial relationships in a largely fantastic (or exotic) universe, or about women and their fantasies, desires, and anxieties (concerning adventurous romance, eternal youth, and murderous husbands) which, quite shockingly, become real.[24]

These women include Joan Wilder in *Romancing the Stone*, Madeline Ashton and Helen Sharp in *Death Becomes Her*, Eleanor Arroway in *Contact* and Claire Spencer in *What Lies Beneath* (2000). Kristin Thompson has charted, in a sequence-by-sequence analysis, *Back to the Future*'s narrative process, and shows just how indebted the film is to classical narrative structures, indicating Zemeckis's wholehearted participation in Spielberg–Lucas Hollywood revivalism.[25] This is not to deny the formal particularity of Zemeckis's work, however.

For example, Zemeckis tends towards the use of a highly mobile camera. While establishing shots from a moving camera are common, Zemeckis employs particularly lengthy examples, and then, when a breakdown into static coverage would be expected, uses movement wherever possible. In *Back to the Future*, although his camera was often static when action necessitated it, when it did not, he tended to incorporate a mobile point of view, known as 'reframing'. Consequently, 42 per cent of the shots in *Back to the Future* include appreciable movement. Marty's journey to school in 1985 is all moving shots (which underlines the mobility he achieves using the skateboard), and the musical number, even Marvin's call to Chuck Berry, is composed virtually entirely of moving shots, as is the scene where Marty and Doc retrieve the hidden DeLorean. Zemeckis is also fond of the slow dolly-in, often to connote increased intimacy or intensity, and (in *Back to the Future* in particular) eeriness, in such instances as Lorraine's 'I don't know, but I'm gonna find out', and Marty's uncomfortable writing of the warning letter to Doc.

New Hollywood had made much of using camera movement as a method of transferring the point of view from location to location, which, in the place of edits, made for shots of relatively long duration. *Back to the Future*, by contrast, with an average shot duration of 5.5 seconds, reflected a general decrease in average shot duration that had begun in earnest during the 1970s. As David Bordwell points out, between 1930 and 1960, the average shot duration of most films fell between 8 and 11 seconds. During the 1970s, roughly three-quarters of films averaged between 5 and 8 seconds, and during the 1980s this narrowed to 5 to 7 seconds.[26] Although Zemeckis did not seek to make extensive use of camera movement in place of edits until *Cast Away*, *Back to the Future* achieved this low average shot duration in spite of his use of camera movement as the basis for some noticeably lengthy shots. The opening shot lasts for 2 minutes and 6 seconds, a brief insert reveals the pile of dog food, then a further 30-second shot shows Marty's entrance. The later shot in this scene, where Marty talks to Doc on the phone, is 41 seconds long. The lack of incidental music in this 5 minute and 39 second opening scene also directs attention to the visual track (a trait Zemeckis would also take to an extreme in *Cast Away*, which lacks incidental music for its first 70.8 per cent). Other shots that are deliberately lengthened by the decision to use camera movement in place of editing include the coverage of Marty and Jennifer's encounter with Strickland (56 seconds); their ensuing conversation while walking through the square (48 seconds); Doc and Marty's discussion when alone in the school corridor (57 seconds); Marty following George home (35 seconds) and Doc setting up the 'experiment' by the clock tower (30 seconds). After all, if 'New Hollywood' was Hollywood under the invited influence of the techniques of the various post-war European 'new waves', then 'New New Hollywood' was a resurgence of classical Hollywood that was nonetheless unwittingly influenced by the techniques of New Hollywood.

Zemeckis's fondness for camera movement also meant making extensive use of focus racks. For example, rather than cutting from the close-up of Doc's remote to a medium shot of the DeLorean reversing, the camera merely racks focus from the one to the other. The urgency of the alarm clock going off on the dashboard is underlined by the use of a focus rack rather than a cut. Just after Marty is hit by Lorraine's father's car, George sits up into the frame (which involves a quick double focus rack away from Marty onto George and then onto Lorraine's father). The beginning of the culminating race-against-time sequence is signalled by a shot that

begins at a steep upward angle on the clock tower, rapidly refocuses on the foreground when Doc walks into the shot, and then tilts down to become level as he walks away from the camera, panning left and right as he moves about in anticipation. The loudhailer of the 'battle of the bands' judge is deliberately allowed to loom out of focus, as is the Libyan 'nationalist's' rocket-launcher, both for comedic effect.

The unacknowledged influence of New Hollywood's heightened camera movement (although movement was also notable in the work of Alfred Hitchcock and Orson Wells) was also retuned by Zemeckis: he made use of camera movement in three dimensions rather than maintaining any equivalent of a human observer's standard head height. The camera moves above and around the DeLorean when it first backs out of the van, it cranes down from above to show the DeLorean covered in ice when it returns from the first time experiment, and it cranes up and tilts down when Marty inserts the connecting hook. It is persistently placed at the height of the DeLorean's bumper when it is in motion, and, linked to the skateboarding and dancing, frequently returns to this position to follow characters' feet. Zemeckis also often 'allows' his camera to lose track of its subject, which usually, in the place of a cut, leaves the camera on the next relevant part of the *mise en scène*. When Lorraine and her friends run off at the sound of the bell, the camera backs away to initially track them but then stops so as to let them leave the shot, which leaves the shot composed on Doc. Although the introduction to Marty in the first scene follows the common filmic pattern of establishing a protagonist by 'listing' shots of their body parts before finally revealing their face (we see his eyes 1 minute and 35 seconds after first encountering his body), the first of these, showing Marty's lower legs as he enters Doc's workshop, is taken from 'dog height' (appropriate given the preceding action with the dog food) and framed in this way only incidentally (at least overtly), because this is where the camera was positioned at the end of the previous event (the dog food can falling into the bin).

Zemeckis's camera movement also, at least overtly, wanders away from the main action (another New Hollywood trait). After the camera shows Marty's lower legs entering Doc's workshop, it then allows him to walk out of shot, instead following his skateboard as it trundles along the floor to bump into the plutonium case.

When Marty leaves, he is again ignored and disappears, out of focus, in deep space, while the plutonium is kept in focus in the immediate foreground, filling just under half of the frame. Before the audition, the last of the shots following Marty to school allows him to leave the frame when it 'notices' the Goldie Wilson van, and after the audition, a shot following the now moving Goldie Wilson van allows it to leave the frame to follow Marty and Jennifer. Nonetheless, true to New New Hollywood form, such camera movement is motivated: all these shots reveal pertinent details. The case of plutonium marked 'HANDLE WITH CARE' (and which will not be handled with care) is handled carelessly when Marty's skateboard bumps into it. The film extensively foreshadows future events in this way (events also mostly located in the historical past). When Marty arrives home, the camera stops following him to dwell on the wrecked car, but this is to emphasise what it means for his nascent sexuality. When the camera moves away from Marty and George in the diner to follow Goldie Wilson soliloquising about the possibility of becoming mayor (in a shot that is 26 seconds long), this occurs so that, once the camera returns to Marty, the audience will share his surprise that George is gone. The camera then also briefly lingers in the diner, watching Marty's frantic pursuit of George through the window along with the diner staff, rather than, for example, using an edit to an exterior shot to follow him outside; keeping the viewpoint with the diner staff also serves to express Marty's sense of alienation in 1955.

Zemeckis's frequent use of movement and focus racks also means that actors often have to undertake complex and precise choreography relative to the camera, as in the lengthy shot when Jennifer is consoling with Marty after his failed audition. The 1985 Strickland slowly draws in towards Marty's face, the camera moving closer to them both to eliminate any empty space. When the DeLorean is revving up to drive towards Marty and Doc, and Marty is edging off to one side, the camera moves in to eliminate the gaps on either side and exaggerate the gap between them. Marty's improvised 1955 skateboard turns in the immediate foreground, and the camera follows it with a drastic pan.

In those shots where he did not employ appreciable reframing, Zemeckis often made comedic use of off-screen space. After Doc finishes his obscure reverie about Peabody, he looks at his van and then determinedly exits the frame, leaving a panicked Marty to take his place in a visual augur of things to come. When Biff is about to leave the McFly home, the set-up places him close to the camera and large in the frame; thus, when he leaves both the house and the frame, George is revealed, diminutively, much further away and much smaller in the frame. Marty baffles Lou the diner owner for 28 seconds, throughout which time Lou's body fills most of the frame, so obscuring another customer sitting next to Marty at the bar; when Lou finally moves aside, the reveal on George sitting in exactly the same posture as Marty is all the more comedic. The shot where Lorraine runs out of frame, throws Marty's trousers into the shot, appears in a reflection in a mirror and then vacates both the room and the reflection in the mirror, leaving Marty to fall out of the shot while trying to put his trousers on, is rapid-fire visual comedy.

After bringing Marty down to dinner, Lorraine's mother walks right up to the camera while Marty, Lorraine and the three children eat in the background, and then shouts into close off-screen space for Lorraine's father, who subsequently backs into the frame with the television, a structure that emphasises the strangeness of the technology recently introduced into mealtime experience.

Genre

> *Back to the Future* is a comedy adventure science-fiction time-travel love story.
>
> Robert Zemeckis, 1985[27]

Zemeckis wasn't exaggerating. But *Back to the Future* is not multi-generic in the sense of mere light-hearted irreverence for the supposed mutual exclusivity of genre. He and Gale built together a broad catalogue of implicit and explicit references to established genre tropes. The time-travel concept encapsulated in the title and the poster certainly made claims about *Back to the Future*'s membership of the science-fiction genre, as did such minor details as the electronic sounds that issue when the solely mechanical back door of Doc's

van opens to reveal the DeLorean, and the unexplained smoke that escapes from the DeLorean when Doc opens the door; and, as will be discussed in Chapter 2, the film's trailer allied it to a short cycle of teen-science films. But *Back to the Future* also moves much more widely in the field of genre, far beyond the confines of science fiction.

Timothy Shary, Stephen Prince and Vivian Sobchack are among those who, in spite of the film's overt science-fiction identifiers, categorise *Back to the Future* as a comedy.[28] Slapstick and farce play a substantial part. Michael J. Fox was chosen as Eric Stoltz's replacement for his more overtly comedic physical behaviour. When the DeLorean first disappears, the disparity between Doc's enthusiasm and Marty's incredulity is made comedic by a lengthy shot in which the two repeatedly walk in opposite directions, away from and towards the camera. Visual humour also features in Doc's sincere apology for the crudity of his expertly constructed model. In encounters with both George and Biff, Marty is framed so that he is peeping out from behind them. Alongside Marty's tendency to knock his head on the DeLorean's gull-wing doors, the film also features, as Andrew Gordon has noticed, fourteen instances of people either falling or being knocked down,[29] and is book-ended by two falls by Marty: first, his encounter with the huge amplifier, and last, his fainting out of the frame (a classic slapstick composition) when he meets his improved parents. The more overt, even cartoonish, moments of physical comedy include the glint of Marty's 'cocked' guitar pick; Doc looking down the barrel of the gun that won't work; the twirling of the DeLorean's shed number plate; the puff of dust when the DeLorean is driven into the barn and Biff's pirouette when punched by George. Verbal humour is also prominent.

Dramatic irony, for example, appears early on, in Doc's advice, shortly after the amplifier has exploded, that 'you'd better not hook up to the amplifier, there's a slight possibility of overload', and is shot through the film's 1955 section, including Lorraine's father's promise to Lorraine (about Marty) that if 'you ever have a kid who acts that way, I'll disown you', and Doc's remark to Marty about George, 'maybe you were adopted'.

Back to the Future also has two genre climaxes, the first a romantic-comedy climax in which the geek gets the girl at the school dance, and the second a science-fiction climax featuring the almost impossible task undertaken in the disorienting lightning storm. The film also evokes the Western, in such instances as George grabbing the chocolate milk slid to him down the bar of the diner, and the showdown between Marty and Biff in the main square. There are

The comedic juxtaposition of light-hearted capering with paralysing shock

also buddy-movie elements, centring on Doc and Marty's relationship (which stresses the successful coordination of collaborative action). The two sport matching head injuries in 1955, and a homosocial intimacy far more relaxed than Marty's nervous encounters with women is clearly expressed in the shot when, upon being asked to the dance by Lorraine, Marty retreats back to Doc and leans against him, fitting neatly around his friend.

Marty's performance at the dance also brings the film briefly into the territory of the musical, not just because of the involvement of a musical performance, but also because the number stops the plot for a brief period, a fact that Zemeckis was conscious of when editing the film for time.[30] The overt use of 1950s songs, including The Chordettes's 1954 release of 'Mr Sandman', Fess Parker's 1955 version of 'The Ballad of Davy Crockett' and Etta James's 'The Wallflower (Dance with Me Henry)' alongside Marty's encounters with caricatured elements of 1950s culture, alludes to *American Graffiti* (1973), one of George Lucas's pre-New New Hollywood films, usually regarded as a New Hollywood product. Lucas's soundtrack included popular songs, one for each scene, and most were 1950s hits. Zemeckis, however, chose to make all of this music occur in the story space, further identifying the film with the musical.

This deliberately all-encompassing mixture coheres closely with New New Hollywood's broad attitude to genre. New Hollywood had paraded a revisionist approach to genre conventions, not by disregarding genre but by setting out generic motifs to contradict them or leave them unfulfilled, as in such 'genre' pieces as *M*A*S*H* (war film; dir. Robert Altman, 1970), *McCabe & Mrs Miller* (Western; dir. Robert Altman, 1971), and *Chinatown* (hard-boiled detective drama). New New Hollywood, by contrast, mixed numerous multiple genres. Although, as Michael Allen notes, '[t]here has ... always been a tendency for films to combine diverse generic elements in an attempt to try to offer a broad audience appeal',[31] the New New Hollywood blockbuster piled up genre tropes in no particular pattern, treating genre as content rather than a mode of operating. This was related to the idea that if each genre attracts a relatively exclusive segment of the public, attaching multiple genre tropes to a film would make it more likely to attract a larger audience.[32] Stephen Prince notes, for example, that although the science-fiction/fantasy genre dominated the blockbusters of the 1980s, a major strain of these films also emphasised whimsy and light comedy.[33]

This genre mixture was also, in part, an outlet for Zemeckis and Gale's simple impulse to make films in classical Hollywood genres, an impulse that would manifest itself more explicitly in *Back to the Future Part III*, a Western in an era when the genre had been virtually demolished for its imperialist ideological underpinnings. The principle over which they had bonded with Spielberg and Milius was that crafted storytelling was more virtuous than the apparently pointless transgressions against narrative convention undertaken by the various 'new waves'.[34] Structurally, the film adheres closely to classical Hollywood principles. Marty moves along the classical narrative trajectory of a hero's progress in the face of more and more complex impediments, from the 1955 Doc's initial refusal to believe that either time travel or Reagan's presidency are possible, through the interference of the gang of school bullies, George's refusal to court Lorraine's affections to the race-against-time at the second climax. *Back to the Future* also sought to renew Hollywood practice by distilling, into concentrated form, the classical equilibrium–disequilibrium–equilibrium story formula. Instead of a disequilibrium that merely implies that a negative future might cohere in unspecified future story time, Marty's temporal situation means that the changes to the future resulting from his disequilibrium are changes in a historical present that we have already seen; these are played out immediately rather than implied, as the images of both his siblings fade in the photograph and even his own body begins to disappear, a threat that is even reflected in the score. In the scene when Biff has George in an armlock, the diminishing possibility that George will ever end up with Lorraine means imminent erasure for the protagonist in addition to mere teen failure, and Silvestri accompanies this with an eight-note phrase played repeatedly on two different octaves of a piano, with the lower octave syncopated, generating a sense of the unravelling of reality. The shots of Marty fading away onstage are accompanied by the rapid scraping of strings usually reserved for horror movies. In a reflexive comment on film history, the film also opines that the most thrilling technological and spectacular developments are likely to be those that have been incubated by a man who has isolated himself in his workshop since 1955, the era of classical Hollywood's apparent rescue by the introduction of widescreen, and before the arrival of the back-to-basics technological array, unmotivated protagonists, broken editing rules and location shooting of the French *nouvelle vague* and New Hollywood.

Even *Back to the Future*'s clear science-fiction genre identifiers make overt allusions to Hollywood film history. The two Doc Browns of the movie represent the two major science-fiction permutations of the scientist: the absent-minded benign boffin and the crazed lunatic.[35] The Doc of the 1980s produces functional gadgets, entertainments (i.e. the big amplifier and speaker) and toys (even the time machine is a remote-controlled car), experiments in merely making clocks lose time, and has a sense of humour ('If my calculations are correct, when this baby hits 88 miles per hour, you're gonna see some serious shit') and style ('The way I see it, if you're gonna build a time machine into a car, why not do it with some style'). Absent-minded, he forgets to turn off his equipment, neglects to tell Marty about the possibility that the amplifier will overload and floats off into recollections. This Doc just wants to go to the future to see 'beyond my years' (an allusion to H. G. Wells's Time Traveller), adding the possibility of getting betting information as a joking afterthought. Even his deal with the Libyans is comically irreverent, with its allusion to pinball. By contrast, the Doc of the 1950s is far more remote from the world. When Marty first meets him, the 'Jacob's Ladder' (a high-voltage travelling arc) prominently placed in the background of the shot of Marty with the sucker on his forehead evokes a lengthy history of cinematic representations of the laboratories of hubristic scientists, as does the surrounding smoke and the Doc's attempt to read his mind. Several of the shots during Marty's first meeting with the 1950s Doc are framed from below so that the ceiling fills much of the background, a common composition for suggesting a sense of disorientation in the presence of derangement. This Doc is crazed by the discovery that the time machine works, shouting 'It works!' while a storm brews in the background, in an echo of Colin Clive's 'It's alive!' as Henry Frankenstein in *Frankenstein* (dir. James Whale, 1931). The allusion to *Frankenstein* is also redoubled by the final scene, as Doc dangles from a gothic castle during a storm in an attempt to harness lightning (the town hall, although classical in design, also sports gothic statues). As with such monster-creating Hollywood scientists, Doc's invention becomes a curse. This Doc's absent-mindedness is far from harmless, instead causing damage to his surroundings, including setting fire to his garage. The 'Brown Mansion Destroyed' newspaper headline in the film's opening shot suggests that Doc either destroyed his family house in an experiment or has intentionally burned it down for insurance money, both of which evoke the excesses endemic to the mad scientist. Marty also briefly blunders into a UFO film when he first arrives in 1955. This allusive texture reappears when

the dialogue explains the film's title. Looking and pointing towards (though not at) the camera, Doc promises Marty: 'next Saturday night, we're sending you back to the future!'. Pointing straight at the audience, Doc seems to be addressing *them* with a promise of a time-travel film as a Saturday-night cinema attraction.

The primacy of action-adventure/science-fiction motifs, which *Back to the Future* shared with its contemporaries, may also explain the film's wider generic mixing. Geoff King is not alone in pointing out that, in regenerating the blockbuster during the late 1970s, Hollywood moved away from the mainstay blockbuster genres of the 1950s – epics, musicals and Westerns – and into action-adventure (arguably cultivated from a mere industry-wide tendency into a fully-fledged genre during this period) and science fiction.[36] He ascribes the prominence of these genres to the perception that because film's spectacular qualities could make the best use of the size of the cinema screen, films heavy in spectacle would be most effective in generating audiences. In 1982, Steve Neale opined that *Raiders of the Lost Ark* 'uses an idea (the signs) of classic Hollywood in order to promote, integrate and display modern effects, techniques and production values'.[37] Similarly, in *Back to the Future*, recognisable genre tropes provide safe touchstones on which to display the film's foregrounded effects shots (e.g. when, in the last shot, the car is thrown right at the audience) and its relatively complex foray into temporal movements other than the normal passage of time, notably Marty's return to 1985 before he left. In particular, given that optical effects techniques were still not yet even close to producing photo-real images, they featured heavily in films that were intended to look fantastical, including *Ghostbusters*, *Weird Science* (dir. John Hughes, 1985) and *Highlander* (dir. Russell Mulcahy, 1986).

In mid-1986, even though Noël Carroll saw such films of the past year as a clear example of Hollywood's simple return to the genres of the 1930s–50s (these included *Back to the Future*, *Lifeforce* [space vampire; dir. Tobe Hooper], *The Goonies* [treasure-hunting pirate-gang adventure; dir. Richard Donner], *Silverado* [Western; dir. Lawrence Kasdan], *My Science Project* [teen-science adventure; dir. Jonathan R. Betuel], *Rambo: First Blood Part II* [war; dir. George P. Cosmatos] and *Real Genius* [teen-science adventure; dir. Martha Coolidge]), which had been in progress, in his view, since the mid-1970s, he added that

[t]his time, instead of churning out simple copies of past hits, Hollywood produced fairly sophisticated confections, larded with in-jokes and arcane allusions to motion picture history. Few in the audience understood those references, but crowds flocked to the new movies – science fiction, Westerns, and other variations on old recipes.[38]

Rather than the playful homage of knowing cineastes, however, the act of stacking together many very different genre conventions could also be seen as part of a larger ideological film-making project. As Andrew Britton argued in his lengthy 1986 critique of contemporary films, 'Reaganite entertainment refers to itself in order to persuade us that it doesn't refer outwards at all.'[39] Spielberg's protégés, in particular, made frequent overt reference to each other's and Spielberg's films. Joe Dante's *Gremlins* includes a reference to the Indiana Jones films, Richard Donner's *The Goonies* contains an

allusion to *Gremlins*, *Back to the Future* references *Star Wars*, the
February 1981 draft of *Back to the Future* opened with a shot of the
climax of *Close Encounters of the Third Kind* (1977) on television, and
Back to the Future Part II includes a reference to *Jaws*. *Back to the
Future* builds a substantial catalogue of popular cultural references
outside film too. Norman Kagan sees the whole trilogy as characterised
by allusions to popular culture, and Vivian Sobchack notes that '*Close
Encounters*, *Time After Time* ..., *E.T.*, *Starman*, *Cocoon* and *Back to
the Future* all show off American popular and "schlock" culture: old
movies and TV series, material artefacts, peculiar cultural habits and
institutions'.[40] Marty's attention to television, which involves
designating certain dated episodes of *The Honeymooners* as classics
and using vocabulary from *Star Trek* as cultural reference points,
resonates with the popular-culture connoisseurship commonly seen as
characteristic of teens. Other popular-cultural references include, in the
1950s, the 1955 Davy Crocket craze, science-fiction comics and the
television series *Science Fiction Theater*, and, in the 1980s, the music of
Eddie Van Halen. Given that the 1980s was the first decade when
video achieved a presence in the majority of American households, it is
significant just how central Zemeckis and Gale made a video recording
to the plot:[41] vital information needed to return Marty to the future is
only gleaned via the videotape he made of the 'experiment' in 1985.
In addition, the 1955 Doc is fascinated with the 1985 video camera's
capacity to rewind, and on returning to 1985, Marty 're-watches' the
earlier part of the film where he fled the Libyans, albeit from a different
angle. Such popular-cultural reference, both explicit and implicit, was a
way of signalling affinity with the 'niche' film audience of teenage
males that New Hollywood had reinforced as the industry's bedrock
(see Chapter 2).

  The tendency towards genre pastiche could, of course, be seen
as an attribute of a post-modern text. Milton Baines's question to
Marty in 1955, 'what's a re-run?', suggests that Zemeckis and Gale
regarded the 1950s as a time before popular culture began, self-
cannibalistically, to consume its own tail. Far from ephemeral,

however, this genre tendency has also had a significant impact. As early as 1986, Noël Carroll perceived that the Spielberg generation had already succeeded in what he saw as a 'revivalist mission'.[42] Collectively, New New Hollywood paid tribute to classical Hollywood genres, plots and scale in a way that exceeded mere reverence for a cinema free of the paranoia of the 1960s and 1970s. These multiple uses of genre are part of what David Bordwell has identified as the 'more classical' or 'hyperclassical' cinema of the 'post-classical' period.[43] The Spielberg–Lucas generation's certainty that a recognisable array of ideas and images called 'Hollywood' had ever existed contributed to Hollywood's survival, both as a 'look' and as a synonym for 'a major social event'. Amblin's basis in the Universal lot has, for example, led to much virtually studio-era in-house production, and *Back to the Future* was a significant instance of this. Realising that their plan to have Marty return to the future at ground zero of a surface nuclear test would be unaffordable, Zemeckis and Gale trawled the Universal backlot for a suitable set that might be used, for free, to stage his return, deciding on 'Mockingbird Square',[44] most famously used in *To Kill a Mockingbird* (dir. Robert Mulligan, 1962), and more recently on *Gremlins*, the first Amblin project. Zemeckis and Spielberg both seem to have been comfortable with using backgrounds that risk looking like sets. *Back to the Future*'s chosen predecessor was also a classical Hollywood product, the opening scene citing two moments from MGM's *The Time Machine* (dir. George Pal, 1960).[45]

Having surveyed the *formal* consequences of *Back to the Future*'s place in film history, we will, in the following three chapters, discuss some major contexts for the film's *content*: teen culture, the backlash against second-wave feminism, recent developments in digital technology, nuclear mythology, theories of time travel and the representation of the passage of time. In addition to the mixture of generic tropes that was characteristic of New New Hollywood, genre features in two more earnest guises in *Back to the Future*, which Chapter 2 will relate to the film's affinity for the 1950s.

2 The 1950s and Teen Culture

The 1950s was the birth of the American teen culture. That was the
first time that the teenager started to rule, and has ruled ever since.

Robert Zemeckis, 1985[46]

Do you really think I oughta swear?

George McFly

Back to the Future and the teenpic

Back to the Future expresses its relationship with the 1950s partly
through its complicated associations with and expressions of
different genres, and particularly the contemporary version of what
Thomas Doherty describes as the 'teenpic' – a film genre aimed at,
about and starring teenagers that was intended to exploit the massive
post-Second World War shift in the composition of cinema audiences
towards mobile, restless youths with disposable incomes.[47] It has
remained one of Hollywood's foremost genres since its inception,
played roles in both creating and reflecting the category of the
teenager, and enjoyed a particularly visible and explicit resurgence in
the 1980s, when the teenpic's exploitation of teen-interest themes
(sex, booze, drugs, rock and roll, delinquency, rebellion and the
difficult transition to responsibility and adulthood) took on a
renewed, if further complicated, vigour. The invention and
development of the cultural category of the teenager itself is closely
intertwined with the rise of the teenpic, and *Back to the Future* both
allegorises and complicates the birth of the teenager in its story and
themes.

The teenpic surfaced in the 1950s, in the wake of economic
shifts that affected the lives of all Americans, but American teenagers
in particular. The maturation of the American post-war economy was

doubly influential on the rise of the teenpic genre: first, the increase in wealth and the consequent upsurge in home and car ownership led to more independence for teenagers, allowing them to stake an increased territorial claim to public sites such as drive-in cinemas; and second, American homes started to be colonised by the television set, which provided free family entertainment without the need to leave the house. With television suddenly able to provide productions to a wide 'general' audience (a role previously occupied by Hollywood films), the drop in attendance at cinemas was colossal – over 50 per cent between 1949 and 1959. So the studios, now unable to compete for the wider audience, had no choice but to start pushing harder to appeal to teenagers, the only group that could still be relied upon to get out of the house to attend screening venues in large numbers. Also, the effect of the 1948 US Supreme Court rulings (the so-called 'Paramount decrees') was to effectively dismantle the apparatus that had provided a long period of complacency and near-monopoly for the major studios. With studios no longer able to own their own chains of cinemas and other exhibition venues, or force theatres to take on packages of cheap, mediocre pictures along with the ones they actually wanted to show ('block-booking'), they could no longer virtually guarantee audience share. Smaller, independent studios – which were often already taking advantage of 'niche' audiences such as teenagers – were able to get their films into more venues and to exhibit more widely as a result, and this helped to fuel demand for teenpics that the major studios would have to learn to meet.[48]

While the teenpic of the 1950s engaged with a teenage audience, it also helped to construct the well-known image of the teenager itself – and especially the rebellious, rock-and-roll obsessed youth – that pervades the contemporary vision of the same. Thomas Doherty identifies a subtle story of the complex emergence of teenage consciousness that is too exhaustive to repeat here, but he highlights a number of landmark cinematic moments that show, in particular, the relationship between the teenpic and popular music:

films like *Blackboard Jungle* (dir. Richard Brooks, 1955) and *Rebel without a Cause* (dir. Nicholas Ray, 1955), while not, for Doherty, teenpics themselves, were a proving ground for teen film appeal, and the blueprints for films both centring around teenagers and explicitly intended to exploit the teenage market.[49] The first major example of these ensuing films was *Rock around the Clock* (dir. Sam Katzman, 1956), which crystallised a generational distrust of authority both on and off screen through the burgeoning craze for rock and roll. The Bill Haley and the Comets song from which the film's title came (and which provided the scaffolding against which the film was constructed) supplied a cheap and convenient way for the film to be promoted on the radio.[50] The song and film co-substantiated, and this moment of the teenager's rock-and-roll birth-cry is referenced by *Back to the Future*'s use of Chuck Berry's 'Johnny B. Goode', which was released in the same year (of which more later).

If the 1950s was the birth decade of the teenpic and the teenager itself, the 1980s saw the genre assume the shape of a more cohesive 'second generation' (a link perhaps analogous to the generational relationship between baby boomers and their then-teenage offspring). The teenpic never 'went away' as such, as the teenager remained a more reliable demographic than any other for the consumption of film, and teenagers were important correspondents of the counter-culture formulae of New Hollywood – but there was a visible leap in the number of explicitly teenage films in the 1980s, and this resurgence also brought with it a number of modifications to the genre. Ostensibly foregrounding and celebrating the licentious aspects of teenage life, films like *Porky's* (dir. Bob Clark, 1982), *Fast Times at Ridgemont High* (dir. Amy Heckerling, 1982), *Revenge of the Nerds* (dir. Jeff Kanew, 1984) and John Hughes's six teen films in the period from 1984 to 1987, including *Sixteen Candles* (1984), *The Breakfast Club* (1985), *Weird Science* and *Ferris Bueller's Day Off* (1986), traded heavily and explicitly on narratives about rampaging teen sexuality, recreational drug use, fashion and resistance to school, cultural conformity and other forms of adult authority. Timothy Shary's analysis of the teen movie asserts that the teenpic experienced a resurgence in the 1980s because of a growing youth irritation with the Reagan administration's post-Carter social dictates. Also, because such counter-cultural movements as punk had failed to really take hold in the US, consumption of teen-oriented culture became a manner of expressing teen politics in a vicarious and paradoxically apolitical way, 'desperate' as American youths were to experience sex and drugs in the way that previous generations of teenagers had managed.[51] The Reagan administration's 'naive "just say no" approach to serious adolescent choices'[52] also induced a deep resentment for authority in America's youth. Jon Lewis's assertion that 'no American youth movement before or since has laid so bare the desperation residing at the heart of the now-failed urban American dream' writes large the biggest single underlying reason for this new form of the teenpic.[53] Nevertheless, with this backlash against Reaganite conservatism finding some form of articulation in the reinvigorated teenpic genre, and this genre representing a far more explicit and extreme version of its 1950s forebear, *Back to the Future* resides firmly at the conservative end of this spectrum. As we will discuss, the film infers a less subversive treatment of teen culture than most of the other teen films of the decade.

So, the teenpic appears at its most strongly defined in the 1950s and the 1980s, the two decades in which the story of *Back to the Future* takes place – making its membership of the teenpic camp seem almost inevitable when its subject matter and cast of 'teenaged' characters is considered. Superficially, it appears easy to slot the film into place as a teenpic; indeed, one whose teenpic credentials are doubled by its iteration of both major phases of the genre. Clear teenpic identifiers perform functions in both the film and its publicity. Jonathan Bernstein refers to *Back to the Future* as part of a short-lived 'teen-science cycle' that also included *WarGames* (dir. John Badham, 1983), *The Last Starfighter* (dir. Nick Castle, 1984), *Repo Man* (dir. Alex Cox, 1984), *Explorers* (dir. Joe Dante, 1985), *Weird*

Science, *Real Genius* and *My Science Project* (in just three weeks in August 1985), *Flight of the Navigator* (dir. Randal Kleiser, 1986) and *SpaceCamp* (dir. Harry Winer, 1986).[54] These films featured stories foregrounding collisions between teenage characters and themes and novel or fantastic technologies. TV promos for *Back to the Future*, though, sold a more licentious, incest-tinged comedy that evoked the more generically stable teenpics of the period: when Universal was advertising the film on television, the most-used extract was Marty's question to Doc at the school in 1955, 'Are you trying to tell me that my mother has got the hots for me?'. The studio acknowledged the difference between the television and cinema audiences, too: one original theatrical trailer for *Back to the Future* signalled the film's membership of the teen-science camp. Marty's sneakered feet and denim-clad legs approach the DeLorean in close-up, then his hands are seen operating the various time-travel-related devices in the interior of the car. With Doc eliminated from the trailer, the time machine was sold as the accidental invention of a teen nerd. In spite of Zemeckis's implicit appeal to the wide audience of the New New Hollywood blockbuster, Universal seemed to have perceived that the main cinemagoers were still the teens-to-mid-twenties male audience of the contemporary teenpic and New Hollywood before it. Insomuch as *Back to the Future* is a rewriting of *The Time Machine*, its modifications were teen-oriented. A small change in circumstances means that someone other than the inventor ends up using the time machine, and this person carries the baggage of life as a teen into the resulting science-fiction events. Some script aspects also anticipated this: for example, Marty's 'time circuits on, flux capacitor ... fluxing', which echoes the humour, endemic to the teen-science subgenre, derived from the implicit mismatching of an overtly fun-loving stage of life with productive scientific objects.

 Back to the Future's relationship to both waves of the teenpic is, however, more complicated than its embeddedness within an existing nostalgic tendency to recall the 1950s. It masquerades as a teenpic in some ways, partly to undermine the newly reinvigorated subversive nature of the genre, and it also includes 'straight' teenpic functions that modify and update the generic/thematic expectations held of teenpics.

Masquerading

The decision to promote *Back to the Future* as a libidinally charged teen adventure was arguably a remnant of Zemeckis and Gale's initial attempt to pitch the film specifically as a candidate for the 1980s version of the teenpic genre (the February 1981 draft of the script sees, among other things, Marty pirating pornographic videos and being invited to a friend's house to smoke marijuana), but the model of the teenpic that remained in the film as it was released theatrically could not easily be classified strictly within that delineation. In other words, because it was a blockbuster dressed in the garb of a teen movie, *Back to the Future* denoted some of the features of the contemporary teenpic, and yet reassembled them in a different configuration, with different thematic and ideological connotations. The outcome of this for the film's representation of the teenager is an image of youth that seems rather more about limiting or containing acts of rebellion than celebrating them (indeed, as Jon Lewis has remarked, the function of the teenpic has often ultimately been about the restoration or rediscovery of adult authority).[55]

In chronicling the birth of rock and roll and ensuring the 1950s segment of the film take place almost exclusively in teenage spaces (the school, the diner, the dance and so on), the sheer celebratory tone of the treatment of the golden age of teenage experience makes *Back to the Future* a kind of meta-teenpic. This tribute extends, though, more to a fear that the pristine nature of the category of the 'teenager' is among those American icons or myths under threat by a more cynical and subversive version of youth consciousness that had developed out of the various counter-cultural movements of the 1960s onwards. The 1980s inheritor of the 'teenager' label – disgruntled by Reaganite conservatism and feeling left out of the perceived excesses of the 1960s and 1970s; (slightly) anarchic, androgynised, punk-influenced – is rejected by the film in favour of

restoring the safer, more wholesome version from the 1950s.
The film's deployment of rock and roll is a particularly useful
example of this: the opening sequence, in which Marty's single power
chord causes the amplifier rig to overload and blow him across the
room, connotes a warning about the destructive implications of
overflowing the 1950s blueprint for rebellion.

This renunciation of the 1980s version of rock and roll is
reiterated when Marty is told that his band is 'just too darn loud' by
a character played by Huey Lewis himself – partly an ironic dig at the
generational difference in aesthetic perception, but also a more
straightforward presence: a reliable, commercial yet youth-endorsed
arbiter of what is 'just loud enough' in contemporary music.
This 'too loud' quality of 1980s rock and roll is never disproven:
Marty's instrumental skill is demonstrated in his 1955 performance
of 'Johnny B. Goode', but his inability to stop himself from pushing
that performance 'too far' into specifically 1980s heavy-metal
gestures – and the pejoratively stunned reaction from a young
audience – signals the limit to which rebelliousness and
nonconformity can be condoned.

The choice of the Chuck Berry song itself (Marty's performance
not only evokes Berry's distinctive onstage dancing, he even plays

nearly the exact same Gibson ES series guitar that Berry played) is
telling in its 'safeness': 'Johnny B. Goode' is so firmly embedded in
the popular-cultural canon that it was actually shot into space in
1977 on the *Voyager* probe's 'golden record' as representative of
American music. While Marty observes that 1955 is simply 'not
ready' for his modifications to this kind of music, actually, as far is
the film is concerned, neither is anybody in 1985: we do not,
ultimately, receive a ratification of Marty's own more radical take on
rock and roll in either decade. It is only ever presented as absurd:
from the exploding amplifier (played with the comically tiny 1980s
guitar), to the use of a snippet of an overdriven harmonic dive-bomb
as aural torture in 1955 (rather than the more tonal content of any
actual songs), to Marty exceeding the 'true' rock aesthetic at the
dance.

There is, overall, an impulse to contain the 1980s modifications
to rock and roll. 'The Power of Love', while energetic and pitched at
a youth audience, is relatively restrained compared to the excesses
that Marty perpetrates in the movie. Indeed, while early in the film
Marty is encouraged by Jennifer to send a demo tape to a record
label, this plot strand disappears – script directions showing him
throw this envelope away before his trip to the 1950s and then

Hill Valley's 1955 teenage population registers its disgust at Marty's over-the-top
performance

retrieve it in the 1980s did not make it into the final cut (the envelope in Marty's hand when he emerges into the living room is a remnant of this): the film's ending rewards Marty with a successful yuppie family instead of a more dangerous rock-and-roll career.

Indeed, one gesture of containment of the post-1950s teenpic seems to come from the film's tendency to draw a direct line of causation between the 1950s and the 1980s: 'problems' in the present (Marty's dysfunctional family; his excessively rebellious understanding of rock and roll and lack of money or a car) can only be 'fixed' by going all the way back to the point at which things started to 'go wrong'. By producing clear relationships of antecedence between 1955 and 1985, the film literally erases from its story space the very existence of the 1960s and 1970s, decades in which a series of significant events prompted dramatic and disruptive cultural changes in the United States: war in Vietnam, the civil rights movement, the Cuban Missile Crisis, the Kennedy assassination, Watergate and Richard Nixon's resignation, and so on.

The potency and hope of the (nostalgic vision of) the 1950s teenager was eroded by real-world messiness and modifications made in the subsequent decades, and, as John Belton suggests is the case with much 'Reaganite' cinema and *Back to the Future* in particular, this prompts an impulse to return to 1950s optimism about the future:

'Reaganite' cinema exploits many of the values and qualities that Reagan himself espoused, as well as the conservative concerns of an emerging, new right – the young, upwardly progressive professionals – the so-called yuppies of the 'me' generation. Indeed, one of the goals of Michael J. Fox [...] in the 1950s segment of *Back to the Future* is typical of the concerns associated with the 'me' generation: he serves as a matchmaker between his future mom and dad and thus ensures his own birth [... .] [These films] feature characters who return to the golden age of the 1950s and come back to the present full of the promise and spirit of this idyllic past, reenergized and ready to confront the future.[56]

Perhaps the most widely observed example of *Back to the Future*'s rewriting of cultural history is its alteration of the origin story of rock and roll, which provides an altered account of the musical genre's emergence by placing the responsibility in the hands of one white teenager. Mark Winokur suggests that Marty's performance of 'Johnny B. Goode' – one of the film's best-known, most iconic scenes, despite its relative unimportance to the film's plot – iterates a desire for white America to feel less indebted to black culture for its cultural structures.[57] Marvin's telephone call to Chuck Berry states the reverse: black debt to white talent. Robert Miklitsch notes that when Marty remarks 'it's an oldie where I come from' (i.e. that it has no history in 1955), the film makes the racially patronising claim that rhythm and blues did not originate with black culture: 'The script's alibi for this startling act of appropriation is, of course, the utterance of the word "spook" earlier in the sequence.'[58] For Winokur, the scene's other main alibi, its comedy, only intensifies its significance:

This comic obfuscation works by reversing a historical trend – pretending that the causation was the other way around. The wish is presented as comic, but the fact that there is a great deal of audience energy cathected to it is probably significant. The rock and roll scene in *Back to the Future* is one of the more popular for audiences to recapitulate.[59]

We see not only that Marty invents rock and roll, but that his performance is ratified in terms of its 'authenticity' by his winning the respect of the all-black band. This validates Marty's performance as 'genuine' and excuses what is essentially a blackface performance. Indeed, Hernán Vera and Andrew Gordon suggest of such moments that 'the white masquerade is rendered acceptable and even comic [...] because it is black-sponsored'.[60]

Another moment where the film rewrites white origination into the history of black social advancement is when Marty influences the 1955 Goldie Wilson to run for mayor of Hill Valley. While we see that Goldie Wilson was mayor in 1985, the emphasis on Marty's influence, and its further iteration of the comic trope of 'reverse causation', lends the Marty-originated path to Goldie's success a sense of authority and 'correctness': it essentially becomes the 'true' version of events. Notably, Marty does nothing particularly concrete to help Wilson become mayor, but just gives him the idea – as if black social advancement was only held back by the inability of black people to realise it was even an option and seize the initiative, rather

than being denied by, for instance, a complex network of cultural barriers and systemic prejudices.

In short, the 'masquerade' seems to take these teenpic genre features and divert them into gestures of rebellion that are no longer rebellious, deifying the 1950s iteration of teenage culture and pushing away modifications made to it by cultural events that occurred between the 1950s and the 1980s.

Functioning

While *Back to the Future* subtly uses the teenpic as a means of both gaining an audience and redirecting the genre's 1980s excesses back into a safer 1950s blueprint, it also functions as a teenpic in various ways. The physical, embodied presence of the teenage characters of *Back to the Future* is certainly concordant with the reinvigorated teenpic: gasping, breathless and clumsy, the hormonally charged awkwardness of adolescence is channelled into a kind of acting performance that, although seeking to be comedic, dramatises the central conceit of discovering the teenager in one's own parents. Apart from such teen embodiment and yearning towards rebellion, sex, drugs and rock and roll, teenpics also represent a narrative within which a teenager battles to achieve an adult sense of consciousness. The teenage subject – that is, the concept of the teenager itself and how it differs from either adults or children – is a relatively novel transitionary figure between those two states. *Back to the Future* not only functions to express this common narrative, but radically exaggerates the discourse. While teenpics tend to focus on the teenage years as a time during which preparation is made for an individual character's entry into adulthood, in *Back to the Future* Marty has to act on behalf of his parents to literally *establish* the adult world. The future, for Marty, is not just a question of an approaching task for which certain skills must be acquired, but one of utterly radical absence – the future is something that he must scramble to literally (re-)enable. Accordingly, the film is replete with forceful images of Marty being confronted by the absence of a

recognisable adult world: the estate where he grew up in the 1970s
and 1980s is simply gone; the mall from whose car park the DeLorean
launches its maiden voyage into time is a farm. This is no mere
'destruction' of the adult world, and there are no remains, debris,
bodies or rubble of a lost future. There is no elsewhere to which the
world of the 1980s could have been moved (if anything, its 'location'
is more a question of 'elsewhen'). The world of the adults of Marty's
original known present has literally been erased by its not having
occurred (a concept persistently reiterated by the presence of the
photograph of Marty's slowly disappearing family).

   This absence of the adult world is further emphasised by the
reversion of the adults in Marty's 1985 life to teenagers in the 1950s
(though arguably even in 1985 they are infantilised, having failed to
properly negotiate their own teenage experiences). This intensifies the
narrative of teen acquisition of adult responsibility: Marty has to
work to adopt the adult consciousness now absent among his
contemporaries, in order to ensure that not only his own adulthood,
but also the notion of a world beyond the teenager, ever comes into
existence at all. Ultimately, of course, Marty achieves adult
consciousness in a fairly stable teenpic fashion, by proving his ability
to move through and affect the adult world in responsible ways

(intervening in life-changing decisions, driving a car, regaining Jennifer). These crises are, essentially, reflective of adolescence itself as a kind of crisis. The premise of this story in particular, though, again serves to concentrate the effects of his achievement of adult consciousness. The time-travel narrative allows an intensification of the positive effects of Marty's making the 'correct' moves through the most slippery years of youth. In *Back to the Future*, rather than an oblique gesture towards a brighter future that we may experience as an audience of a more generic teen film, we are treated to an instantaneous snapshot of the dramatic effects of Marty's success in mastering his youth experience. There is not just *some* evidence of improvement in the lives of those immediately around him, but instant, major changes.

The DeLorean also invokes one of the most robust and persistent features of the teenpic genre – the automobile. In teen films, the car represents both a means of mobility and an escape from the confines of authority, but also provides a device through which the progression from childhood to adulthood can be effected and dramatised. While the DeLorean is not the object of Marty's lust at the film's outset (he has his eye on a Toyota 4×4 that he acquires at the end of the film), Doc Brown's time-travelling car, and its

appearance as a replacement for the destroyed parental car, greatly exaggerates a common trope in teen movies of both the 1950s and the 1980s. Steve Bailey and James Hay read the car in the teenpic as part of a wider discussion of the physical sites 'in which the social identities of youth find articulation'.[61] The teen's ability to move through and between these spaces becomes 'a critical element in the depiction of the teenage experience', which makes the car both a literal and figurative device in the establishment of the teenage subject.[62] The car provides a metaphorical, and in *Back to the Future* literal, means of mobility between childhood and maturity. The crisis and pain of adjusting to the adult world of the car – which, in *Back to the Future*, is instigated only by desperation in an emergency (escape from Libyan terrorists) – constitutes a kind of 'prosthetic puberty', an extra, final stage of adolescence through which Marty must progress towards adulthood. He must, in other words, learn to handle the car and its power in a responsible way. The importance of the car is signalled too by one particular way in which *Back to the Future* works to construct Marty as a singularly teenage subject: his ways of moving through the world – most obviously on a skateboard, but also in more obliquely teenage gestures like kicking open gates, jumping over fences, starting a car by head-butting it – construct him as a teenager rather than an adult or a child. The upright, visible and – when 'skitching' lifts on cars – rather dangerous travel of the skateboard suggests 'teenager', while 'child' tends to be connoted by the bicycle (and 'adult', of course, by the car).

However, the film complicates and retrofits even further the already complex connotations of the teenpic car. Addressing *Back to the Future* specifically, Bailey and Hay highlight the film's advanced adaptation of the teen subject's relationship to these sites: they suggest that Marty exemplifies a member of an 'environment wherein social authority derives more from embodiments of youth as a category of advanced temporal-spatial mobility than from the disciplinary enclosures such as the school, the theatre or the house'.[63] So Marty's relationship with the DeLorean, while attaining and

exaggerating the motifs inherent to the teenpic presentation of the automobile, also overflows that relationship and suggests a new kind of non-linear mobility in the 1980s teen subject. In other words, Marty's ability to subvert time signals a peculiarly post-modern augmentation of the teenage experience, which requires an even greater awareness of the changeable and non-Euclidean quality of the highly technologically mediated contemporary western lifestyle (see Chapter 4).

3 The 1950s Imagined in the 1980s

The main analytical route when considering *Back to the Future*'s
1950s subject matter is an examination of Reaganite nostalgia.
The film's yearning for certain supposedly decayed ideals – such small-
town post-war values of the Eisenhower era as childhood innocence,
the nuclear family and the domestic American dream – have, along
with its Oedipal undertones, attracted the most critical examination.
Stephen Prince writes that *Back to the Future* 'epitomized the
collective yearning for a pristine past that the Reagan years had
defined as a core national aspiration'.[64] Vivian Sobchack, in an
examination expressing a new-found similarity between mainstream
and marginal science-fiction film in the 1980s, suggests that these two
modes of the cinema industry were united by a similar nostalgia,
celebrated 'by the blatant pronouncement of [*Back to the Future*'s]
very title'.[65] The film's treatment of the past strongly positions the
1950s as a lost object of desire. The Hill Valley of 1985 is
suburbanised, scrawled with graffiti, its clock tower broken, one of

Smegma

its cinemas now showing porn, and plagued with such comically portrayed 'fads' as aerobics. Its very narrative circumvents the vast social changes of the period between 1955 and 1985 and renders them obsolete by drawing a clean line of causality from the former to the latter.

Back to the Future's participation in the wider Reaganite amnesia about the 1960s and 1970s is particularly acute in its implicit commentary on feminism. Susan Faludi has argued that the 1980s saw a peculiar double logic appear in popular commentaries on feminism:

Behind this celebration of women's victory, behind the news, cheerfully and endlessly repeated, that the struggle for women's rights is won, another message flashes. You may be free and equal now, it says to women, but you have never been more miserable.[66]

While it is laudable that equality for women has been achieved, the logic ran, this has turned out to be women's ultimate misfortune. The idea that women's liberation has caused all of their problems was pervasively used to charge feminism with the crimes perpetrated against it.[67] Focusing on thrillers and romantic comedies, Faludi identifies the backlash logic in American film from 1987. *Back to the Future*, however, contains a germinal version of this logic. Rather than merely showing an image of a non-functioning contemporary family, the film roots this situation in George's failure to assert himself, against Biff in the present and over Lorraine in the past. In the original timeline, George initiates their relationship by being the victim (hit by Lorraine's father's car) rather than the wielder of physical force. A man damaged by outside forces, 'like a little lost puppy', can only produce the kind of marriage in which his wife is an alcoholic. Although the film does not overtly relate this emasculation – either in 1985 or 1955 – to feminist history, the degeneracy of the Hill Valley of 1985 is expressed both implicitly and explicitly as its feminisation. Many downtown buildings are unused because life has moved to the pure shopping experience of the out-of-town Twin Pines Mall, so signalling the draining influence of this commonly feminised social activity on the integrity of the town. Among those downtown buildings that *do* remain in use, Lou's Diner has become Lou's Fitness Center. This emasculated 1980s is then fixed by a journey to a decade when backlash politics were both successful and much more overt, when, in the years following the Second World War, women in America were compelled to abandon 3.75 million industrial jobs (and when, fuelling the perceived need for an assertion of the maleness of the workplace, 2.75 million women entered the workforce in clerical and administrative positions).[68]

The year 1985 is also improved, as Marsha Kinder points out, because Marty's novel presence in 1955 arouses erotic desire in Lorraine that then leads to a happier marriage when displaced onto George.[69] In line with the common teenpic trope of introducing the older generation to the benefits of new teen values, the more intense sexuality of the younger generation radically improves the lives of the parent generation. The shot of George and Lorraine turning away from their front door while Marty and Jennifer kiss is an image of the older generation condoning the sexuality of the younger. In the original 1985, Lorraine and George have no physical relationship, and Lorraine takes responsibility for this lack when she denies over the dinner table that she ever parked with boys when she was Marty's age. The improving effect of Marty's presence is to alter this marriage to include the sexual agency of its female constituent. This is not to claim that Zemeckis and Gale were championing the fulfilment of female sexual urges in line with such post-war texts as Robert Kinsey *et al.*'s *Sexual Behaviour of the Human Female* (1953) and William Masters and Virginia Johnson's *Human Sexual Response* (1966), or asserting, in line with such early twentieth-century instructional works as Marie Stopes's *Married Love* (1918), that female sexual enjoyment is necessary to a happy marriage, or even implying that female sexual enjoyment is only productively employed when reproductively employed – i.e. expressed towards the known husband. In the original series of events, George's presence in Lorraine's life protects her from Biff. When this is altered by Marty's accidental interference – the interference of an influence from the future – she is almost raped. Expressed outside the known parameters of the marriage to come, female sexual agency attracts a rapist. Indeed, while Zemeckis and Gale laboured to find a way to bar incest from Marty and Lorraine's menu (hitting on the line, 'when I kiss you, it's like I'm kissing my brother'),[70] they seem not to have felt an equivalent urge to cage the spectre of rape. Their aim, apparently, was to position the female protagonist in a situation of intense and sexual danger that would mean that she would beg for help. The question most used in the television advertising, 'Are you telling me my mother's got the hots for me?', steered the viewer away from the Oedipal drama, in which the mother is the unknowing focus of the lust of the son, but only by evoking the reverse. Female sexuality is out of control, a liability to *itself*, if not directed towards the family.

In addition, the fact that the young Lorraine even has a sexuality functions as proof of female hypocrisy (i.e. the hypocrisy of her 1980s self), and interprets real-world feminist gains (by the 1980s) in speaking out against rape and asserting women's control over their own bodies as a mere senseless increase in female prudery. Lorraine's advice against sexual availability prompts Linda to observe that this means she will probably never meet anyone, again echoing the common backlash accusation that feminism meant the end for the procreation of the species. Notably, in his one film to make explicit reference to the various social revolutions of the 1960s, *Forrest Gump*, Zemeckis dramatised the achievement of women's liberation as the achievement of the freedom to contract AIDS.

Bob Gale has described *Back to the Future* as 'a story of a kid who teaches his father how to be a man',[71] and it was certainly not unique in seeking out restored male authority figures. The last of the six characteristics of the Reagan-era films that Robin Wood diagnosed with the 'Lucas–Spielberg Syndrome' in 1986 was

'Restoration of the Father': 'One might reasonably argue that this constitutes ... the dominant project, ad infinitum and post nauseam, of the contemporary Hollywood cinema, a veritable thematic metasystem embracing all the available genres and all the current cycles, from realist dramas to pure fantasy'.[72] Restoration of the father meant restoration of the implicitly errant mother. In *Back to the Future*, ultimately Marty has to adopt a position in which he is less masculine than his father, so that the 1950s can be looked back on as a time of giants from which the 1980s are a fall precipitated, in backlash logic, by feminism. This is underscored by Lorraine's remark that 'I think a man should be strong, so that he can stand up for himself, and protect the woman he loves, don't you?'. The film's logic is that in order to establish future satisfaction for 'woman', the father has to reassert physical authority over the mother. Marty's part in this lies in experiencing similarity with his father. Richard Maltby suggests that *Back to the Future* could be placed in a mid-1980s genre grouping, which also included *Trading Places* (dir. John Landis, 1983) and *Big* (dir. Penny Marshall, 1988), in which characters occupy identities other than their own.[73] Similarly, Marsha Kinder places *Back to the Future* in a mid-1980s genre grouping of father/son age-reversal comedies, also including *Like Father, Like Son* (dir. Rod Daniel, 1987), *Vice Versa* (dir. Brian Gilbert, 1988) and *Big*.[74] In *Back to the Future*, father and son are interchangeable within 'the patriarchal order that empowers them both',[75] Marty coaching his father through the difficulties of dealing with the opposite sex, and both insisting 'I just don't think I can take that kind of rejection'. As with all of these surrounding films, this patriarchal interchangeability, figured dramatically as disequilibrium, serves as the basis for an improved equilibrium, and the improvement undoes gains implicitly rooted in women's enhanced ability to make decisions.

We would, however, like to complicate the neatness of nostalgia as a model for understanding the film's concerns. While the film's yearning for that lost moment of 'perfection' is indeed explicit, *Back to the Future* expresses more specific sentiments and concerns about the 1950s that have their origins in equally specific sentiments and concerns about the 1980s, mostly addressing the position of technology and cultural ideas about the future.

'Erased from Existence': Digital Denial

Back to the Future draws upon science fiction as a way of enabling its core premise: a teenager meeting his parents when they were his age. This science-fiction heritage is tempered, though, by a curious relationship that the film seems to have with the contemporary technologies both of the 'real world' and of cinematic visual effects. Many science-fiction-inflected films of the period were keen to embrace the excitement and imaginative weight surrounding the burgeoning pervasion of the microprocessor and the digital computer, either by dealing with them directly in pre-rendered sequences of hypermediation via computer graphical interfaces (*TRON* [dir. Steven Lisberger, 1982], *WarGames*, *Weird Science*, and so on), or by simply saturating the film with visual effects appropriating the novelty and the 'magic' of digital technologies, and computers in particular: *Star Trek II: The Wrath of Khan* (dir. Nicholas Meyer, 1982), *Flight of the Navigator* and *The Last Starfighter* all foregrounded in their appeal a large proportion of conspicuous digitally created effects. Films like *TRON* and *Weird Science* fetishise the computer within their stories as a producer of quasi-magical fantasy spectacle, and *Flight of the Navigator et al.* have at the core of their visual appeal a number of scenes that are completely digitally generated, and which 'show off' the use of the computer as a mode or modifier of visual production. *Back to the Future*, on the other hand, takes a different approach. While the special effects shots are part of the film's draw as an action blockbuster, they are optical rather than digital, and indeed do not self-advertise as the products of novel technologies: visual effects shots are spectacular but used sparingly, and recall the model and set work of *Star Wars* rather than the computer-generated smoothness of *TRON*.

Perhaps even more significantly, the 1980s that we see in *Back to the Future* is, rather than filled with state-of-the-art gadgets as one might expect, mainly saturated with cobbled-together versions of technologies from the 1950s. Doc Brown's automatic dog-feeding contraption in the opening sequence is both a caricature of an assembly line and a 'Heath Robinson' assemblage of mod cons like the electric can-opener (first introduced commercially in the 1950s by Walter Hess Bodle, a garage inventor not unlike Doc Brown); the room-filling guitar amplifier and cabinet setup that Marty

overloads and destroys bristles with large Dymo-labelled metal knobs and analogue gauges resembling those of much older technologies than the more commonplace plastic-cased solid-state amplifiers of the 1980s.

Indeed, the sheer size of the setup defies the progressive trend of technological miniaturisation seen in the wake of the 1971 emergence of the microprocessor. The flux capacitor itself is, on a conceptual level at the very least, a mere modification of an early electrical component. The capacitor dates from the mid-18th century, the era of the discovery of the nature of electricity (one of Doc Brown's idols, Benjamin Franklin [1706–90], had a hand in developing it), and became mass-produced with the dissemination of radio after 1895. Even the Doc's modification to it dates from 1955, not the 1980s. Peculiar to *Back to the Future*'s treatment of technology, too, is what seems to be the almost total absence of computers and digital technologies. While many contemporary films (*TRON* and *WarGames* in particular) effect a *mise en scène* saturated by microcomputers and their imagined potential, *Back to the Future* achieves its science-fiction foray without featuring any digital computing technology whatsoever. The 'fantastical' technologies attached to the interior of the DeLorean were all aerospace components, and the car's closest candidate – the 'time circuits', with numeric keypad and segmented digital LED output – resemble the single-purpose instrument technologies of aerospace (such as an autopilot panel) rather than the more versatile monitor of a digital microcomputer.

The complete absence of recognisable computers from any of Doc's various laboratories is particularly baffling. One would assume that a figure meant to embody the cutting edge of technological exploration would be taking full advantage of advances in devices so closely knitted into modern scientific endeavour, technologies that were, in the early 1980s, commonplace both inside and outside of those communities. This outright rejection of the computer in any recognisable form is, of course, partly a function of the film's being set mostly in the 1950s, where digital information technologies

occupied no visible place in everyday life, but the absence of these technologies in the 1980s is conspicuous given its focus on high technology. The absence of computers when there was no avoiding them in other science-fiction contemporaries seems a particularly stubborn sign, and may be suggestive of a number of emerging concerns about those technologies.

Back to the Future was released following a series of 'cybernetic' films, including *Blade Runner* (dir. Ridley Scott, 1982),

The interior of the DeLorean

TRON and *The Terminator* (dir. James Cameron, 1984), but rejects the issues that those films began to address: *Blade Runner*, in particular, based on Philip K. Dick's 1968 novel *Do Androids Dream of Electric Sheep?*, explores the subjective breakdown in the categories of human and machine, brought about by the existence of android 'replicants' who believe they are human. The film demonstrates ways in which traits traditionally seen as unique to human beings – empathy, free will and mobile thought, and emotions such as love – could be found in machines that might one day emerge from the digital revolution beginning to take hold in the 1980s. Showing the dwindling of the list of traits that, ostensibly, humans possess but machines do not, the film uses the android as a way of examining dubious assumptions at the basis of conventional understandings of the human subject. Machines and other ostensibly non-human subjects, according to the logic of *Blade Runner*, shape us even as we shape them; we cannot take for granted an inherent essence of 'humanity' that is unique and transhistorical. *TRON* and *The Terminator* do this in more explicit, fearful and less subtle ways, positing intelligent machines as a dangerous potential usurper to humanity's dominance, or even its survival. *Back to the Future*'s treatment of technology is considerably more subtle and normative:

along with its omission of contemporary information technologies, it ensures that technology is seen as the product of human invention rather than the opposite. The film's celebration of the figure of the American inventor in the form of Doc Brown epitomises this. While highly eccentric, he is always depicted as the source of the inventions we see in the film, and the responsibility of mastering and controlling those technologies is one of the only ethical issues for which he accounts. As Zemeckis has remarked,

Bob Gale and I believe that there is a tradition in American folklore about the crackpot inventor, who builds things in his garage … so we wanted to build a machine but we didn't want it to be NASA's machine; we didn't want it to be the government's machine; we wanted it to be his.[76]

In fact, the film effects a kind of 'reverse-retrofitting' in its portrayal of technology. While 'retrofitting' denotes taking an old technology and augmenting it with novel components, *Back to the Future* is intent on the opposite: taking 1980s technologies and bolstering them with elements from the 1950s. The amplifier setup is an obvious example of this, but the DeLorean is the film's centrepiece of reverse-retrofitting. The lightweight stainless-steel 1980s car that had already been a commercial failure (though chosen for its resemblance to the 1950s image of a UFO) is 'improved' by pipes, wires and anomalous chunky components, and its spectacular steam-belching spoilers-cum-exhaust assemblies recall the mechanical, steam-cooling processes of nuclear power.[77]

This desire to recall older, heavier, industrial, analogue technologies – and then literally bolt them onto the somehow inadequate and flimsy technologies of the 1980s – is ultimately compounded by the steampunk aesthetic seen in *Back to the Future Part III*, wherein the once-again failed DeLorean ends up being propelled by a coal-fired steam locomotive. The sheer visibility of the technological processes involved is telling in itself: the need to show technologies that operate in a way that is understandable in terms of

simpler, more tangible physical processes shows a certain dissatisfaction with how the computerisation and miniaturisation of technological and scientific processes (and their abstraction into digital code) seen in the wake of the microprocessor puts them beyond immediate lay comprehension. By resurrecting an older aesthetic for displaying technological wizardry, a clear visual language is maintained that helps relate the narrative events on screen, and the problems of relating scientific practices that had become increasingly computer-aided (and, perhaps, visually dull) in the real world (as tackled by *TRON* or *WarGames*) are sidestepped, with the industrial, valves-and-transistors aesthetic of the 1950s given precedent. Reverse-retrofitting takes place on a more abstract, cultural level too: specific and fashionable technologies of the 1980s are generally mocked as pointless until they are assigned a more visible 'use' that is concrete and immediate. Marty's stylish puffer jacket is met with confusion in 1955 Hill Valley, as it is mistaken for a more obviously useful technology (a life jacket), while the empty, absurd commercial value of 1980s brand names is lampooned by the teenage Lorraine's assumption that the words 'Calvin Klein' stitched onto Marty's underwear represent a more functional labelling of his name on the garments. The portable hairdryer and Walkman that are taken back to the 1950s remain nothing but indulgences until Marty finds a use for them as torture devices.

Back to the Future's near-total elision of digital information technologies and its insistence on 'taming' and retooling the necessarily present (and often 'feminine') technologies and products of the 1980s with more immediate, physical (and indeed more 'masculine') uses is arguably a symptom of concerns over the direction that technology had taken since the golden age of the

1950s: away from the visibly powerful, physical presence of the hydrogen bomb, and towards the permeable, androgynising passivity of information in the form of the digital bit. The film's treatment of technology, then, reflects concerns about a certain 'feminisation' taking place both in technology and in society in general. There is also a clear need to re-subject dangerously 'lively' technology, a milder expression of the aforementioned fears seen in *The Terminator* or *Blade Runner*: Marty invents uses for his objects perhaps as a curative for information technologies' threatening ability to imply that humans are as much a function of technology as the opposite. Linked to this is the film's valorisation of the figure of the inventor – Doc turns to the memory of 'Tom' Edison in a time of crisis to reinforce the historical continuity of 'great men' – those who invent, rather than who are invented by, their work.

Another facet of the film's debt to the cultural expressions of the 1950s is its tendency to resurrect specifically 1950s visions of the future. When Disneyland opened in California in July 1955, the first three of its five 'lands' – Main Street USA, Tomorrowland and Frontierland – expressed America's three main stable myths. These three myths also underpin *Back to the Future*, in the form of the lost perfection of Hill Valley (Main Street USA), the electrical technologies that Doc builds into a car designed to look like a UFO (Tomorrowland) and the further virgin territory discovered by the capacity to travel in time (Frontierland). Bob Gale has remarked that even before he came up with the idea of encountering one's parents when they were teenagers, he and Zemeckis 'had always wanted to do a time-travel movie [...] that took place in a future as seen by the 1939 World's Fair, that had everything wrong in the future'.[78] In the first (February 1981) draft of the film, Marty so significantly changes the past that, on his return to the future, the American people are universally driving flying cars, living in streamlined 'aerodynamic' houses, cooking by push-button, being served by robot butlers, writing with mind-controlled pens, employing and using safe, limitless power generators, and enjoying virtually no inflation (Biff

earns fifty cents an hour, and the monthly fuel bill is two dollars). In the finished version, there are significant remnants of this: Doc's mind-reading device, although a failure, seeks to realise a peculiarly 1950s vision of the future. The 1985 segment, in spite of the minimal nature of Marty's changes, is still modelled to the future of the 1950s: the automatic can-opener writ large as the automatic dog-food dispenser, the device for flicking the on-switch of the television and the flying DeLorean of the film's final shots. Indeed, the unseen future of 1985 from which Doc returns at the finale seems to be the precise future of the 1950s, with flying cars and home fusion reactors ('Mr Fusion').

The valorisation of the figure of the lone inventor also speaks to a fondness for a 1950s vision of the future; Zemeckis and Gale's determination that the time machine should be invented by a private inventor can be seen as a reflection of the general American distrust of federal government, but it also alludes to the American attitude towards the space race. Early Russian 'victories' in the space race suggested that a centralised communist state could deploy resources more effectively than states under other forms of social organisation, and that any attempt to match these achievements meant being un-American. In *Back to the Future*, the Americans get to win the space

'Live in the Home of Tomorrow ... Today!'

race twice. First, by opening up a further frontier: the fact that Doc has been working on the time machine since the 1950s implies that if the Americans lost the space race, this was because they were preoccupied with something harder and better. Second, by alluding to the achievements of centralised power as meagre in comparison to those going on in garages throughout America, the investment of promise and power into the individual is ratified, with invention coming not from a complex network of social forces, but a single, driven individual.

The Atomic Kid: The Return of Golden Age Nuclear Confidence

> Are You Telling Me This Sucker's Nuclear?
> No no no no no! This sucker's electrical.
>
> Marty and Doc

In addition to working to override contemporary concerns about technology, the film's nostalgia for 1950s technological ideas and futures also reflects a recent increase, in American society, in one strain of technology: the nuclear. Andrew Britton and Robin Wood have both suggested that, when approaching the topic of nuclear weapons, the primary function of popular American science fiction or fantasy 'entertainment' cinema such as *Star Wars*, *Raiders of the Lost Ark* and *Star Trek II: The Wrath of Khan* was both to assuage widely held public fears of mismanagement of the nuclear deterrent, and to discourage enquiry on the topic altogether.[79] This reading is indeed persuasive. However, rather than seeing *Back to the Future* as a palliative for a general sense of nuclear anxiety, we perceive several levels of engagement with nuclear discourse. The above-mentioned films do indeed appear to reflect and respond to a certain popular uneasiness with nuclear power, and this anxiety was compounded in its visibility by a resurgence of films explicitly concerning global nuclear catastrophe (*Mad Max 2* [dir. George Miller, 1981],

WarGames, *The Day After* [dir. Nicholas Meyer, 1983], *Threads* [dir. Mick Jackson, 1984] and *The Terminator*, for instance) that is easy to map onto the arrival of aggressively conservative heads of state on both sides of the Iron Curtain: Ronald Reagan in the USA in January 1981, and Yuri Andropov in the Soviet Union in November 1982. *Back to the Future*, however, seems to evoke a new-found or rediscovered *ease* in the popular imaginary in co-existing with the bomb. This ease of showing off the power of nuclear technologies occupies a telling position in relation to both those earlier films that gestured towards the issue of nuclear armament in an oblique but reassuring way, and those that treated it with a sense of nothing less than impending apocalypse.

The first few years of the 1980s had engendered a glut of films with the dual ideological function of both defending the viability and safety of the nuclear weapon (when wielded by the United States, of course)[80] and deflecting attention from the issue altogether by providing films of 'entertainment' that close down commentary on their social-political contexts by their very nature.[81] If we were to seek examples of this kind of 'assuaging' of fears about the bomb, we would not need to look further than some of the biggest movie events of the late 1970s and early 1980s. And, indeed, the message in those films appears to be one of both reassurance and encouraging obliviousness. As Robin Wood writes:

The fear of nuclear war [...] is certainly one of the main sources of our desire [...] to be reassured, to evade responsibility and thought. The [...] sense of helplessness – that it's all out of our hands, is continually fostered both by the media and by the cynicism of politicians [. ...] In terms of cinema, one side of this fear is the contemporary horror film, centered on the unkillable and ultimately inexplicable monster [... .] The Michael of *Halloween* and the Jason of the later *Friday the 13th*[... .] The other side is the series of fantasy films centered on the struggle for possession of an ultimate weapon or power: the Ark of the Covenant of *Raiders of the Lost Ark*, the Genesis project of *Star Trek II*, 'the Force' of *Star Wars*. The relationship of the two cycles [...] might seem at first sight to be one of diametrical opposition (hopelessness vs. reassurance), yet their respective overall messages – 'there's nothing you can do, anyway' and 'Don't worry' – can be read as complements rather than opposites: both are deterrents to action. The pervasive, if surreptitious, implication of the fantasy films is that nuclear power is positive and justified as long as it is in the right, i.e. American, hands.[82]

However, by 1985 there was a shift in the public perception of nuclear power of all kinds that rendered such performative gestures of reassurance unnecessary – and replaced them, in *Back to the Future*, with a film *explicitly celebrating* the quasi-magical power of the atom. In spite of the fact that 1985 was the year when the number of nuclear warheads in America, and in the world, reached an all-time high,[83] the Reagan administration had managed to foster a sense of nuclear optimism. Of course, this attitude to nuclear power (and weapons) had already been most vividly displayed in the 1950s, and this sense of innocence and naivety – even fun – about the bomb is one that *Back to the Future* works hard to resurrect.[84]

The 1950s contained a number of culturally significant moments in the emergence of an era of unmatched, supreme American confidence in the positive future heralded by nuclear

'Handle with care' seems a comic understatement when talking about plutonium

power. President Harry S. Truman's decision to detonate atomic bombs above Hiroshima and Nagasaki in August 1945 had arguably brought the Second World War to a decisive end. American military superiority had thus been both confirmed and demonstrated to the world, and the detonation of the first hydrogen bomb in 1952 – many times more powerful than the original bombs dropped on Japan – seemed only to reinforce this picture of American military might. In addition to this, the same atomic power that was at the basis of these weapons was promising a new, clean, seemingly infinite source of energy. The first warship powered by a nuclear reactor, the *USS Nautilus*, went to sea in 1954, apparently proving the widespread adaptability of the technologies of nuclear energy. The popular fantasy of the level to which this power could feasibly be ported – and thus manifest itself in everyday life, rather than just in military applications – was exemplified by Ford's 1958 Nucleon concept car: a vehicle powered by a small nuclear reactor in place of an internal combustion engine. This was never built, let alone sold to the public, but it serves as a potent illustration of the imaginative power of this atomic 'golden age'. Hollywood films often reflected the 'magic' of the atom: a vague understanding of nuclear radiation's role in mutation engendered films such as *The Gamma People* (dir. John Gilling, 1956), in which gamma rays are used by a Soviet scientist to make children super-intelligent; or *Timeslip* (dir. Ken Hughes, 1956) – whose tagline was 'The Man with the Radio-Active Brain!' – and in which a scientist affected by radiation from his experiments is permanently pushed seven-and-a-half seconds into the future. Spiderman, in his original comic-book storyline, acquired his powers through being bitten by a radioactive spider. There was also a plethora of films in which the awesome power of the atom is blamed for the creation (by mutation) of monsters. The popularity of the Japanese film *Godzilla* (dir. Ishiro Honda, 1954) is an obvious marker of the perceived 'magical' potency of radiation, but American films continued to reflect a parallel fascination: *The Day the World Ended* (dir. Roger Corman, 1955), *The Phantom from 10,000*

Leagues (dir. Dan Milner, 1955), *The Cyclops* (dir. Bert I. Gordon, 1957) and *Monster from Green Hell* (dir. Kenneth G. Crane, 1958) all feature monsters produced by radioactive mutation. *Back to the Future* itself pays explicit homage to this trope by featuring *The Atomic Kid* (dir. Leslie H. Martinson, 1954), another radioactive superhero film, at the town cinema in 1955 Hill Valley.

This obsession displays a sense of awe at the power of radiation. Yet the technology's widespread permeation seemed inevitable in a society where the market for futuristic consumer goods had exploded with everything from televisions to electric can-openers. Atomic power, in short, had taken on a kind of fantastic, magical quality, but one modified by the progression towards a domestic atomic future.

The peak of this 1950s nuclear confidence, though, passed rapidly, along with its playful celebration of the atom. This shift came about, in part, because of further developments in global nuclear politics that made the atom seem somewhat less 'friendly' than previously. The perceived assurance of the untouchable power of the United States' unique arsenal was shattered in 1955 when the Soviet Union detonated its own first hydrogen bomb. This was followed rapidly by the Soviet test launch of an intercontinental ballistic missile in August 1957, and the surprise launch of Sputnik 1 in

The spectacular importance of atomic power

October of the same year, a double blow to confidence in the superiority of American technology. Important too was the emergence of the new doctrine of nuclear deterrence as a political strategy and global reality. The beginning of the 'Age of Deterrence', wherein the nuclear bomb's awesome destructive capability could be seen to put an end to large-scale war through pure fear of escalation into global apocalypse, has been dated to 1954, 1955 or 1956 by various scholars.[85] The year 1955 also saw the formation of the pro-western Baghdad Pact in February, the signing of the pro-Soviet Warsaw Pact on 14 May, and the East–West meeting of the Geneva Conference from 8 May to 21 July – all events signalling, as Robert J. McMahon writes, 'both sides' tacit recognition of the existing status quo in Europe – along with the implicit understanding that neither would risk war to overturn it'.[86] So, while this emerging stalemate introduced a certain sense of security that arguably allayed some fears about the likelihood of the *use* of nuclear weapons themselves, this de facto admission of the atom's unparalleled destructive power nevertheless provided a point at which nuclear naivety simply no longer seemed tenable. There was, then, a shift in public perception of nuclear weaponry as the 1950s drew to a close, reflected by both the founding of organisations such as the Campaign for Nuclear Disarmament in London in 1957 and the circulation of a number of propaganda texts designed to reassure the American people that the bomb was in safe hands, and that even if the worst happened, America would be ready. Such texts include Disney's 1957 book and film *Our Friend the Atom*, which sought to divert attention back to the constructive domestic uses of nuclear power, glossing over its military origins in the Manhattan Project.

The year 1955, then, seems to be a fair point at which to locate the beginning of the end of the golden age of nuclear innocence and the point at which the realities of the Cold War begin to sink in, all of which makes *Back to the Future*'s choice of time-travel destination telling. Indeed, while Zemeckis states that the decision to set the 'past' parts of the film in 1955 were purely logistical,[87] it is clear that he and Gale were not willing to move beyond that date, even though nearly four years passed between the first draft of the script and the beginning of production, and even though they nailed the 1980s date to the advancing historical present. If 1955 represents a turning point in popular perceptions of atomic power, then it also represents the last moment at which that post-war nuclear ease was defensible. As we discuss presently, *Back to the Future* recalls that playful and naive fascination with the power of the atom in multiple ways. However, our sense is that *Back to the Future*'s eagerness to relive that sense of ease is not simply linked to nostalgia. A number of specific political and cultural shifts in 1980s America could account for a renewed sense of optimism about nuclear power.

When Reagan came to power, it was on the back of a campaign promising tax cuts and less government intervention in the lives of citizens, but also a shift in foreign policy away from détente and towards antagonism with the Soviet Union. The new Republican administration's robust defence strategy signalled a desire to bury perceived military failures such as the Vietnam War in favour of restoring a sense of confidence in American military superiority by finding solutions to nuclear and economic stalemate. One of the more conspicuous symptoms of that attitude was the jump in defence budget: during the Reagan years, as Dean Baker notes, 'military spending had risen by nearly a third, from 4.7 percent of GDP in 1979 to 6.2 percent in 1986'.[88] But perhaps the most tangible expression of this desire to restore American military superiority was Reagan's televised 23 March 1983 announcement of plans for the Strategic Defense Initiative (SDI), an ambitious network of ground- and space-based technologies designed to neutralise the threat of Soviet nuclear attack by detecting enemy missiles in flight and destroying them in space with satellite-mounted laser and kinetic weapons. Although pejoratively dubbed 'Star Wars' by sceptics, this system nonetheless did seem to integrate itself into the popular consciousness as at least superficially plausible. For example, SDI very quickly made its way into film narratives. By 1985, a number of

Logo for the Strategic
Defense Initiative

films had already made reference to the system: *Real Genius* and
Spies Like Us (dir. John Landis, 1985) have narratives ordered
around the top-secret and cutting-edge nature of an SDI-like system.
Other films represented responses to SDI, if less directly: Constance
Penley reads the Artificial Intelligence 'Skynet' of *The Terminator* as a
fictionalised representation of a pervasive defence network
resembling SDI.[89] Such contemporaries as *Best Defence* (dir. Willard
Huyck, 1984) overtly advocated enhanced military spending on new
technologies by dramatising the dangers of corner-cutting, while
others such as *Short Circuit* (dir. John Badham, 1986) envisioned
possibilities for military spending beyond the nuclear impasse.

   With the promises of SDI, America's vast stockpile of nuclear
weapons – for so long made impotent by the impasse of mutually
assured destruction – was no longer so useless. The possibility of
security provided by a sense of inarguable American military
superiority rather than stalemate, not seen since before the Soviet
Union detonated its first hydrogen bomb, once again seemed within
reach. Accordingly, the atomic itself – no longer, with American
control seemingly assured, just a malevolent force waiting for its
moment to destroy mankind – took on an imaginative weight similar
to that it had possessed in the early days of the Cold War.
The renewed (and yet, like that of the 1950s, fleeting) confidence

generated by this shift is, we argue, reflected in the unique attitude towards both nuclear power and nuclear weapons in *Back to the Future*. If *Raiders of the Lost Ark* is a parable about the need for the United States to both possess and bury nuclear technologies, insisting simultaneously on their existence and their non-use, *Back to the Future* finds domestic and magical uses for nuclear technologies. In seizing plutonium intended for use in a bomb by 'Libyan nationalists', Doc Brown reasserts that older discourse on nuclear power: that the material originally intended for use in a weapon can (in the hands of an American) be harnessed for benign purposes. The quasi-magical quality of nuclear power reflecting that 1950s atomic golden age, resurrected by this new-found Reaganite confidence, runs through many of the film's main elements.

The 'radiation suits' that Doc and Marty wear on the night of the first test of the time machine seem more ritualistic than functional: emblazoned with radiation-warning trefoils on their backs, the garments seem to suggest a charm-like ability to ward off radiation rather than the more mundane reality of how such protective gear tends to work in real life (which is, we understand, more about preventing the inhalation of radioactive particles than preventing the penetration of radiation into the skin). This trope is, of course, not unique to

Back to the Future, but it resurrected a misconception about radiation common in similar narratives in the 1950s: that its permeation can be controlled with the correct ritualistic invocations. Marty is further reassured that the car is 'lead lined', and while lead has wide applications as radioactive shielding, its place in fiction and the popular consciousness as a cure-all or defence against radioactive permeation arguably places its protective properties in a rather gnostic mode.

This then brings us to the clearest tangible object signalling this resurrected sense of nuclear confidence in *Back to the Future* – and also the most complicated to read. The DeLorean – with its onboard plutonium-fuelled nuclear reactor, which in turn generates electricity for the flux capacitor that, to paraphrase Doc Brown, 'makes time travel possible' – is a complex assemblage of nuclear and electrical fantasies both eventually enacted by the film and thwarted by its production process. The idea of a nuclear-powered car alludes to the Ford Nucleon as a distillation of 1950s fantasies of the potency and portability of nuclear power. The DeLorean's 'Mr Fusion' device seen at the very end of *Back to the Future*, which turns garbage into fuel, is a riff on the domestication of nuclear technology, effected by referencing the cheerfully glib nomenclature of 'Mr Coffee': a popular home coffee-maker. Before it is given this convenient augmentation, though, the car's (and the film's) relationship with the radioactive remains rather mystical: while Zemeckis and Gale remark that they researched nuclear reactors when conceiving the DeLorean's augmentations (hence the exhaust steam), and Doc Brown insists that the time machine is 'electrical' (just requiring a vast quantity of electricity to run that could only be efficiently generated by a nuclear reactor), the discourse on radiation that remains is one where *radiation itself* still possesses a supernatural potency. The decision to make the car 'electrical' seems to be more about a reluctant production decision (though one very cleverly exonerated by later rescripting). The time machine of the 1981 draft ran directly on radiation (hence the need to place it at the site of a hydrogen bomb test in the Nevada desert to get Marty back to the future). The vast

financial cost of producing this effect was, according to Zemeckis and Gale, the main reason why this ending was changed and the time machine altered to run on electricity so that a lightning bolt could take the place of the nuclear explosion. Yet the lightning continued to evoke the magical understanding of the nuclear, in that the magical account of electricity that was popular during the 1800s was imported to stand in for the impractical magical account of radiation.

In addition, the final version of the film sheds several remnants of paranoia that attached to earlier drafts. The 'Professor' Brown of the 1981 script is killed not by terrorists but by agents from the Nuclear Regulatory Commission who track him down by detecting the radioactive trail of his stolen plutonium using Geiger counters, which expresses an appreciation of the dangers of fissile material. By 1984–5, however, this suspicion had lessened, with the plutonium of the finished film posing no threat except that associated with the rogue elements trying to get hold of it. Zemeckis and Gale also disposed of early dialogue in which a schoolteacher soliloquises on the dangers of nuclear war.

So, *Back to the Future* manages to evoke parallel generic heritages in its treatment of the nuclear and of electricity, and the former seems a result of confidence produced in a unique and fleeting moment of 1980s cultural history. We see this confidence more directly as the basis of several of the film's comic moments – the 1955 Doc Brown's observation that in 1985 he and Marty must be wearing radiation suits 'because of all the fallout from the atomic wars' is marked as an absurd and paranoid concern; the moment is played for its evoking of pleasure in the audience, whose inherent hindsight that a war has *not* happened is coupled with a sense that the threat of nuclear war has actually passed, or is, at least, passing. Thus, not only does the film treat nuclear power as instrumental to the DeLorean's ability to travel through time, humorous moments emerge from the film's treatment of characters who show concerns about the atom that the narrative positions as retrograde.

4 Film and Time

Time travel in film

Back to the Future features several common time-travel motifs. The dream was the common time-travel method in literature before H. G. Wells introduced a mode of transport in *The Time Machine* (serialised January–May 1895), after which devices gradually replaced dreaming. Although Zemeckis and Gale were firmly resolved to follow Wells in using a device rather than a dream to move their protagonist in time,[90] the dream motif nonetheless features strongly. The key component of the time machine is, for example, the product of an unconscious and quasi-supernatural experience: Doc envisions the flux capacitor in 1955 only as the result of a blow to the head that renders him temporarily unconscious. Much like the dreaming time travellers of Mark Twain's *A Connecticut Yankee in King Arthur's Court* (1889) and Ford Madox Ford's *Ladies Whose Bright Eyes* (1911), Doc has an experience as a result of becoming unconscious that is nonetheless real; a trauma-induced hallucination is also a major scientific discovery. Although Marty's belief that the time he spends in 1955 is a dream (for which he finds three separate explanations) is used to exaggerate his shock – at seeing the empty space where the family home should be and in finding himself in his teenage mother's bed – the dream motif reappears in earnest at various points in the film, including the choice of The Chordettes's version of 'Mr Sandman' to allude to his initial reaction to the flavour of 1950s Hill Valley.[91] Indeed, this music, which the viewer initially has cause to assume is merely the soundtrack's expression of Marty's bewilderment, switches to diegetic (i.e. story-space) sound when an eyeline match shows Marty looking at a speaker mounted on the wall outside the record store, indicating this as the source of the music. Thus, an experience that the viewer initially assumes alludes to Marty's state of consciousness becomes a real experience.

The equally established time-travel motif of the frontier also shapes the film. The unsettling experience of open fields in place of Lyon Estates in 1955 expresses, in part, the urge, embedded in most time-travel narratives, to discover new frontiers. Just as *The Time Machine* had supplied a new frontier for British imperial consciousness at a time when there seemed to be no land mass left untouched by European expansion, time travel re-emerged in the early Reagan era to imagine horizons other than the 'iron curtain', as *Star Trek* had with its own 'final frontier' in the 1960s. Wyn Wachhorst noted in 1984 that in the preceding decade, time-travel films had increased by over 50 percent relative to the rise in total science-fiction films.[92] Contemporary time-travel films included *Time after Time* (dir. Nicholas Meyer, 1979), *Somewhere in Time* (dir. Jeannot Szwarc, 1980), *The Final Countdown* (dir. Don Taylor, 1980), *Time Bandits* (dir. Terry Gilliam, 1981), *Timerider* (dir. William Dear, 1983), *The Philadelphia Experiment* (dir. Stewart Raffill, 1984), *The Terminator* and *My Science Project*. *Back to the Future* resonated so closely with Reaganite sentiments that Reagan invoked the movie in his 4 February 1986 State of the Union Address: 'Never has there been a more exciting time to be alive, a time of rousing wonder and heroic achievement. As they said in the film "Back to the Future," "Where we're going, we don't need roads."'[93] Cyberspace, extensively spatialised in such contemporary films as *TRON*, manifested the same urge to imagine new frontiers. These imagined frontiers both expressed the scale of enduring American frontier myth and sought to enhance its reach. Even leaving aside supposed blanket Reaganite nostalgia, time-travel films expressed, as Wachhorst argued, an attempt to 'reinstate the magical, autocentric universe of the child ... while retaining the reality projected by rational, individualised consciousness',[94] which resonated with Reagan-era optimism about America's role in the seeming stalemate of the Cold War.

Time-travel films, in particular, also tend to figure the process of time travel as a kind of birth or rebirth. In *The Terminator*, the journey back in time is 'painful, like being born', and renders time traveller Kyle Reese naked and prostrate on arrival in the past, where he must learn to engage with an unfamiliar world. In both *La Jetée* (dir. Chris Marker, 1962) and its remake as *Twelve Monkeys* (dir. Terry Gilliam, 1995), the protagonist is propelled naked into the past and witnesses himself as a child, 'becoming' that child by dying in his sight. In *Primer* (dir. Shane Carruth, 2004), time travel involves crawling into a collapsible box and becoming unconscious, and infantilises time travellers, rendering them unable to write. In *Los cronocrímenes* (dir. Nacho Vigalondo, 2007), the bumbling lead is sent an hour into the past by a time machine that appears in the form of a vat of viscous fluid, and flops out of the vat dripping, weak and unable to talk. Although the sequels would modify this, *Back to the Future* figures time travel as a kind of traumatic rebirth. Marty regresses when he travels to the past: although he is now in possession of a machine that allows him to travel in four dimensions, not only does it lack the necessary fuel for time travel, its petrol engine also inexplicably fails, and, because he has even been parted from his skateboard, he has to walk the signposted two miles from Lyon Estates to Hill Valley. This contrasts strongly with 1985, when the skateboard had enabled him to shift between distant locations. The flux capacitor also alludes to the process of birth, its outline evoking the arrangement of vagina and fallopian tubes, which makes entering and using the DeLorean roughly equivalent to employing the ostensibly magical generative power of the female reproductive system.

Another reason for the proliferation of time-travel films in the early 1980s lay in changing understandings of space. The treatment of time as a discrete, knowable and 'solid' fourth dimension seems to resonate with concerns about a gradual disintegration of the concept of spatiality itself, a side effect of the pervasion of digital information technologies in the 1980s. As Vivian Sobchack argues, science-fiction

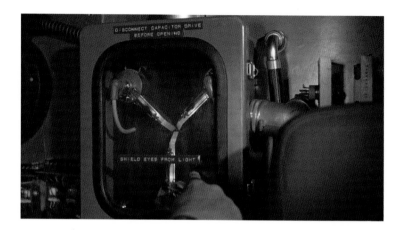

cinema of the 1950s focused on outer-space travel, treating it with 'an aggressive and three-dimensional thrust', with space being 'semantically inscribed as "deep" '.[95] She suggests that the proliferation of information technologies and the surge in the screen-simulated experience in the wake of a widespread adoption of digital technologies challenged the confidence in this perceived depth:

To a great degree, [spatial depth] has become flattened by the superficial electronic 'dimensionality' of movement experienced as occurring on – not in – the screens of computer terminals, video games, music videos, and movies like *Tron* […] and *The Last Starfighter* … space is now more often a 'text' than a context. Absorbing time, incorporating movement, figuring as its own discrete event, contemporary space has become experienced as self-contained, convulsive and discontiguous.[96]

While other films were starting to reflect a shift in the understanding of space because relationships with digital technologies were becoming less linear and more reciprocal, *Back to the Future* treats both space *and* time as 'solid'. Zemeckis and Gale insisted on using a model of time travel where moving in time would not also automatically move the time traveller to another geographical point (and drew on this for comedy in all three films in the franchise). By writing time as a dimension analogous to the three dimensions of tangible 'real-world' experience, the film conveys a sense that if three-dimensional space is under threat from digital fragmentation, that lost cohesion must be recouped in a new axis. This is a particularly convincing phenomenon when related to the clear absence of recognisable computers or other digital information technologies in the film (see Chapter 3). Keeping time solid and knowable as a kind of space, of course, provides a useful shorthand for communicating a complex and potentially confusing storyline, while also alluding affectionately to the spatial aesthetics of 1950s science-fiction cinema.

If information technology has flattened space, it has also, Sobchack argued shortly after *Back to the Future* was released, spatialised time. Production designer Larry Paul has admitted that he sought to give the 1955 segment of the film a 'period' look because, as it was such a recent historical period, there was a risk that it wouldn't look like the past.[97] For Sobchack, the *mise en scène* of *Back to the Future*

conflates and homogenizes temporal distinctions to a spatial 'nowhere' in time [...] that has no connection with 1955 as a 'real' historical past. In both the 1980s and the 1950s, Marty inhabits a nostalgically imagined, romantically generalized American small town. Stripped of historical referents and significant temporal specificity, it appears abstract and highly stylized. [...] This refraction, this softening of the film's vision of a 'real' historical past, is an effect of the postmodern spatialization of time into something(s) visible. It is also an effect of living in an almost totally mediated society in which existence is most significantly experienced indirectly – in the pseudo-events/objects of images, simulations, and spectacles.[98]

The primacy of space means that historical time is incidental, unimportant, with no influence on whether one is experiencing *this* or *that* small town. A thirty-year time change puts Marty in exactly the same place, his uncanny experience of the past deriving as much from the sameness of 1950s Hill Valley as from its difference (Biff is already the kind of person to make 'what are you looking at butthead?' asides while bullying George, and is already performing the 'your shoe's untied' trick).

A spatialisation of time underscores Zemeckis and Gale's particular iconography of time travel. In detailing *how* a time machine might work, they openly followed Wells, who had emphasised that he saw time as an axis just like the three spatial dimensions by describing a machine capable of moving *only* on a temporal axis.[99] To move the time machine in any of the spatial dimensions, it is necessary for both The Time Traveller and Doc Brown to transport the time machine physically; hence, Zemeckis has explained, Doc's solution of building it into a car.[100] Nonetheless, the time machine of the film (although not of earlier drafts) still has to be moving spatially (at 88 miles per hour) in order to be able to move temporally in the first place. This is linked to a larger language of time travel, which, unable to describe temporal 'movement' directly, codes it spatially. For example, in spite of the choice not to have the DeLorean take some time to disappear from the present (one production design idea visualised it disintegrating out of the present front to back) but rather to make time travel instantaneous, the covering of ice on the car when it reappears implies, against the evidence of Einstein's clock, that the DeLorean has been somewhere – a freezing non-space – for a brief period. A spatial language of time travel also surfaces in Christopher Lloyd's explanation, to Marty, of 'when' Einstein and the DeLorean have gone. When Doc/Lloyd says, 'I sent him into the future', he gestures in the direction in which the car was driving, which is also directly away from the camera.

Another force behind this tendency towards spatialisation was the influence of a recent development in quantum physics. Among the burgeoning time-travel subgenre, *Back to the Future* was exceptional, in that it alluded to the phenomenon of time dilation as an explanation for time travel, specifically in Doc's use of two initially

synchronised but then desynchronised digital clocks to test the time machine. Although the image was likely unconsciously placed, it echoed the Hafele–Keating experiment of October 1971. In the first substantial component of his Theory of Special Relativity, the 1905 paper 'On the Electromagnetics of Moving Bodies', Einstein had proposed that the duration of any given event is not invariant from one observer to another, but depends on the relative speeds at which each observer is moving. Someone sprinting will experience the passing of time very slightly faster than someone standing still. The Hafele–Keating experiment was carried out to establish the extent of this variation of temporal experience between observers moving at different velocities. Physicist J. C. Hafele and US Naval Observatory researcher R. E. Keating placed four atomic clocks on commercial airliners so that they circumnavigated the world twice, one eastward, with the earth's rotation, and one westward, against it. Hafele and Keating reported that, relative to a stationary atomic clock, the travelling clocks gained an average of 273 +/– 7 nanoseconds over 80.3 hours when travelling against the rotation of the earth, and lost an average of 59 +/– 10 nanoseconds on the stationary clock over 65.4 hours when travelling with the rotation of the earth.[101] This experiment demonstrated, Hafele and Keating claimed, that it was possible for observers to pass through time at different speeds on the basis of the difference in their velocities. Although *Back to the Future* continues a proud fictional tradition by involving no theory of *how* time travel is made possible, the requirement that the DeLorean reach a specific speed to travel through time echoes this Einsteinian idea that altering one's position in space also means altering one's position in time. Time dilation also appears in the idea of having Marty experience the passing of a week while, for his contemporaries in 1985, no time passes at all. The film even signals the relevance of

Isaac Newton's 1985 disappearance

Einsteinian ideas to Doc's work, not just in the name of his dog, but in his pertinent predecessors. On the wall in Doc's house in 1955, Einstein is accompanied by framed pictures of Isaac Newton, Benjamin Franklin and Thomas Edison, whereas in his workshop in 1985, Newton has been jettisoned from this crew. In directing both set-dressing and framing, therefore, Zemeckis and Gale mutely imply that a movement from Newtonian physics to Einsteinian relativity was essential to producing a time machine.

Oedipus's Family

Among *Back to the Future*'s many characteristics, its overt Oedipal dynamic has attracted the most critical and scholarly attention. Marty's unwitting rivalry with his own father, his unknowing primal encounter with his own mother in her bed (the key scene reprised by the two sequels) and his plan to reunite his parents by becoming a sexual aggressor towards his mother constitute one of the most explicit Oedipal narratives in modern cinema. The son/mother relationship was identified as Oedipal by contemporaries.[102] Just a few days after its release, J. Hoberman remarked that 'Marty is nothing less than an American Oedipus who learns to conquer his desire for his mother [...] and accede to the rule of the father.'[103] Although both Zemeckis and Gale had long wanted to make a time-travel film, Gale's 'chance' encounter with the notion of meeting his own father when he was a teenager did not automatically make for a time-travel narrative (a magic de-ageing plot produces the same situation in *17 Again* [dir. Burr Steers, 2009]). Time travel was the extra ingredient that would make Marty the same age as his mother as well. While Zemeckis and Gale have remarked that they came up with the 'when I kiss you, it's like I'm kissing my brother' line to guard against the Oedipal implications of Marty taking his father's place at his first meeting with Lorraine, this fireguard of supernatural wrongness was only necessary because Zemeckis and Gale had made the choice to pursue a plot with Oedipal implications in the first place.

Moreover, a storyline in which Marty interferes with his
parents' first meeting only necessitated that he prevent George
from being hit by Lorraine's father's car and so have to introduce
the pair in another way to restore his own birth. They could,
for example, have made Marty change the past by delaying George
at the diner for so long that he didn't climb the tree before
Lorraine's father drove under it. To decide that Marty should get
hit *instead* of George was a deliberate choice to unfold the plot

'... like I'm kissing my brother'; Lorraine scrutinises Marty's underwear

along the lines of the son's eviction of his father for the affections of his mother.

Andrew Gordon sees *Back to the Future* as the most overt version of the Oedipal narrative that for him underpins, in sublimated form, most time-travel films. In contrast to *The Terminator*, for example, 'in which a man sends his father into the past to ensure that his father will impregnate his mother', in *Back to the Future*, 'the heroine and hero no longer stand in for mother and son but *are* mother and son'.[104] Gordon details the extent of the film's Freudian drama: for example, Marty is stuck in the Oedipal phase because he has not yet been able to identify with his father (who is too weak) and repress his desire for his mother (who is overpowering). Lorraine also prevents Marty's exit from the Oedipal phase into adulthood by disapproving of his adult relationship with Jennifer. Biff manifests Marty's Oedipal hostility towards his father and sexual desire for his mother, and only through embarking on a magically impelled journey to adulthood can Marty triumph over this desire for his mother, a triumph that requires his father to punish the representation of the son's desire for his mother, and through which Marty achieves the influence over his surroundings of an adult.[105] One possible explanation for this particular association between the Freudian Oedipal narrative and time-travel films is that when films move a character from the present into the historical past, that character experiences the historical past as their personal present. Experiencing, in the present, that which is normally safely embedded in the past evokes the return of the repressed, the experience of lust for the mother and hostility towards the father that the establishment (around age four) of the Oedipus complex (according to Freud) universally enables the man child to repress.

As Jay Ruud has pointed out, the film is Oedipal not just in the sense of dramatising a son's accidental sexual involvement with his mother, but as a rewriting of Sophocles's *Oedipus the King* (*c*.429 BCE). Like Oedipus, Marty attempts to avoid the obvious hazards strewn before him, but in doing so succeeds only in provoking those

very hazards as if predestined. He unintentionally encounters his father and, just as unintentionally, is drawn to his mother's home, which leads him to become the object of Lorraine's attentions and endanger his own existence. By being locked in the boot of the band's car, he causes Marvin Berry to cut his hand and so be unable to play at the dance, meaning that even though George and Lorraine are already back together, they may not have the dance that cements the union with their first kiss. Sophocles's Delphic Oracle, who prophesies that Oedipus will kill his father and marry his mother, also appears in the figure of Doc Brown (who, like the Oracle, has visions, including the flux capacitor), issuing warnings that Marty ignores to his detriment. The film, of course, also reverses several aspects of Oedipus (as Hoberman noticed), with both Marty and Doc changing destinies that seem unavoidable.[106] Rather than feeling erotic desire towards his mother, Marty is able to provoke erotic desire in his mother that ultimately improves the family.

The explicit, and explicitly sexual, Oedipal narrative of *Back to the Future*, Gordon also suggests, is a manifestation of an enduring and distinctively American drama in which a protagonist who desperately resents the home has their wishes fulfilled, only to be forced to confront the nightmarish consequences of this and then to

Marty's Oedipal desires terrifyingly resurrected

find that the home has endured.[107] In *Back to the Future*, as in *The Wizard of Oz* (dir. Victor Fleming, 1939), *It's a Wonderful Life* (dir. Frank Capra, 1946) and *Star Wars*,

there is a scene in which the hero returns to find his or her family home changed dramatically for the worse: Dorothy's home is empty; George's home has been vacant and crumbling for decades and his children were never born; Luke's home has been burned down and his aunt and uncle killed; and Marty's home is a construction site.[108]

All characters experience alternative realities in which the urge for the family to disappear is satisfied. 'Perhaps it stems from our revolutionary origins,' Gordon suggests, 'or from our pioneer restlessness, but Americans are ambivalent about home and family.'[109] The journey back through time can thus be seen as an expression of Marty's prototypical inner resentment of the state of his family in 1985, time travel serving to destroy the family, first by placing him in a time before it has happened and then by leading to circumstances that cause it never to be. Although the 1955 Hill Valley is structured as a lost paradise compared to its 1985 equivalent, Marty's first experiences of 1955 are also intensely unsettling (Alan Silvestri's suddenly very loud score emphasises this). By copying the composition of the earlier shot of the 1985 Lyon Estates, the shot of the same place in 1955 imagines utter absence. Marty then finds that deleting the family is also deleterious to himself. Finally, the family reasserts itself, and not just in the sense that Marty has to resurrect it to save his own life. A subtext of *Back to the Future* is that Marty's family is preordained. In seeking to achieve Marty's first narrative aim – returning to 1985 – Marty and Doc together successfully effect the necessary changes in their surroundings. In seeking to bring about his second narrative aim – uniting George and Lorraine – Marty not only exerts influence solely through the unintended consequences of his actions (inadvertently bringing about the Biff/George confrontation), even this influence proves insufficient.

Although George and Lorraine have been brought together by George overcoming Biff, and although Marty is providing George and Lorraine with music to dance and kiss to, he still begins to fade out of existence. The restoration of his family to history only occurs because George chooses to push Dixon (the ginger interloper) violently to the floor and take Lorraine back. (In this direct iteration of causality, there is no question that Lorraine will merely refuse Dixon, in spite of the fact that she would obviously want to.) Thus while, in his relationship with Doc, Marty is an agent in his surroundings, his family has a life of its own, sorting itself out as a kind of natural phenomenon, hence the appearance from nowhere of the 'like I'm kissing my brother' line. The film asserts the naturalness of the heterosexual nuclear family, the early scene in the diner even featuring a physical intimacy between Lorraine and George when the former is ostensibly infatuated with Marty.

Thus, while the film might seem to provide a fantasy of an alternative to the nuclear family in the adventure narrative structured around Marty's and Doc's fortifying exploits in the realm of spectacular science, this non-familial relationship merely leads Marty

Subtle markers of George and Lorraine's preordained intimacy; Crispin Glover's remarkably sinister performance

to become a more empowered member of the family, able to benefit it by serving as a conduit for outside influence. The extra-familial 1985 Doc, for example, is the origin of Marty's lesson, delivered to George, that 'if you put your mind to it, you can accomplish anything', a line of which Marty is reminded in 1985 by the similarly extra-familial Jennifer.

Back to the Future exhibits particularly neat examples of the tight plotting that marks Zemeckis and Gale's films. For example, the date to which Marty travels – 5 November 1955 – is the day when Doc first envisions the core component of the time machine *and* the day when George is hit by Lorraine's father's car; while the day that he returns to the present – 12 November – is the night of the dance that unites his parents *and* the night of the storm that stops the tower clock. In this bracketed time period, Marty, it is quickly established, effectively has until the clock stops to repair the disequilibrium. However, rather than merely evoking the race-against-time that it emphasises stylistically in the climax during the lightning storm ('Look at the time! [Doc points at the huge illuminated clock] You've got less than four minutes!'), the still ticking clock emphasises Marty's continuing ability to influence events after he has prevented himself from being born. From their earliest work on the script for *Back to the Future*, Zemeckis and Gale gravitated towards the 'grandfather paradox' (a term first coined by author René Barjavel in his 1943 novel *Le Voyageur imprudent*): if it is possible to change events in the past, should a character travel back in time and prevent one of her/his ancestors from reproducing, then their own birth will have been prevented and, as they don't exist, they would have been unable to travel back in time to interfere with that ancestor. Zemeckis and Gale's version of the grandfather paradox is, however, slightly modified. First, although the changes Marty effects in the past cause him not to exist, they do not in turn cancel the trip to the past during which he made these changes. In the modified history (playing itself out in the photograph), where Lorraine and George don't kiss at the dance, Marty came from nowhere, had some brief adventures in

Hill Valley and then disappeared onstage at the dance. Second, the consequences of the paradox – the McFly children disappear from time – do not play themselves out instantaneously, only gradually altering from potential to real, thus giving Marty time to make a second spate of changes. Both differences implicitly insist on the validity of the category of the individual by demonstrating the individual's power to change her/his surroundings. Marty's changes are actual even if they ought to prevent his ever existing (importantly, the 'branching universe' theory that would resolve the paradox is not introduced until the sequel, even though Zemeckis and Gale cited it in the epigraph to the February 1981 draft),[110] and they are only a gateway to the potential for more changes. The text certainly seeks to correct Lorraine's belief that her meeting with George 'was meant to be', first by showing that it could easily have been anyone else, and then having Marty's influence produce the union. Marty is also an instrumental individual, in that he is impervious to change himself. His room in 1985, for example, is exactly as he left it, in spite of the fact that he will have had a very different upbringing from the first version of history.

We would, however, add two qualifications to Gordon's argument. First, although the film makes Marty the cause rather than the consequence of his own family, by making the reunion and improvement of Marty's family the unanticipated result of his actions rather than the actualisation of his intentions, it denies him credit for these changes. Second, there is a further category of Marty's influence on the past. While he changes events from their known historical course, he also effects events that constitute a part of known history (the 'causal loop'). In the former category, Marty kills one of Peabody's pines, thereby altering the name of the mall later built there, improves (albeit unintentionally) his parents' marriage and motivates Doc to acquire a bullet-proof vest. In the latter category, Marty originates the skateboard and rock and roll, determines his own name, causes Goldie Wilson to run for mayor and (although this is understated) invents the time travel that got him there by both

showing Doc that his scrawled drawing was worth developing and
how to do so. Zemeckis and Gale's decisions about which category to
apply to which type of event are very telling. Although the film
demonstrates that an individual can successfully shape her/his
surroundings, Marty's alterations don't include anything communal –
the ways that teenagers move in urban space, dominant musical style
or even local political leaders – but are restricted to the isolated world
of his friends and family. This expresses the idea, particularly strong
in the US, of an individual instrumentality that is guaranteed to be
neutral because it is isolated from political motivations. The family,
as noted above, also exercises a measure of immunity to this
instrumentality.

The Time-sense of Cinema

Back to the Future, as with any film, describes time, both by
combining many small records of time into a new forward-moving
present, and by alluding to the passing of time in elements of its *mise
en scène*. In such instances as the mound of dog food under the
automatic dispenser in Doc's workshop, which gauges the amount of
time that he has been away at about a week, pieces of time that the
film cannot show are measured through prompting the viewer to
make appropriate assumptions.

   Back to the Future is also abundant with allusions to time.
Clocks are the main component of Doc's workshop, he was hanging
a clock when he fell and experienced the flux capacitor vision, he
wears three watches, hangs from a clock at the film's climax and
asks Marty, when he is late, 'do you have no concept of time?'.
This catalogue of allusions, it seems, is placed merely to emphasise
the theme of time travel. However, references to the normal passing
of time are symptomatic of concerns that plague all film-makers. If a
film were to show, without any explanation of the link, one scene
including a clear indication of the time in the story space, and then a
second scene clearly set in the past of the first scene, the viewer
would be forced to choose between two alternatives: a) the film is

showing the memories of a character as they are being recalled in the continuing present, or b) the film has made the equivalent of a grammatical shift from the present tense to the past tense, providing backstory not through exposition in the present but through moving into the story's past and simply showing it. The majority of such shifts in narrative film are accompanied by cues that instruct the viewer to make the first assumption. Instances in film history where the film cues the viewer to make the second type of assumption are very rare (they include *Pulp Fiction* [dir. Quentin Tarantino, 1994] and *Memento* [dir. Christopher Nolan, 2000]). This is because such non-sequential ordering of plot time in the film's time (i.e. the time that the film takes to be shown) jars with the very common perception that the time in a filmic story space passes in tandem with the time in which the film is being shown. That is, while a literary author has access to clear grammatical methods that allow them to pause the story's 'present', shift into the past of that 'present' to detail a previous event and then return to the exact moment 'paused', film can only improvise equivalents of these on an ad hoc basis. The established convention in film for showing a memory, the flashback, keeps the viewer in the present, and this is signalled by having the recall of these past events take up present time – that is,

they are memories recalled in the present rather than a shift into the story's past.

The continuous present tense of cinema means that it must deal out forcible iterations of the 'now' being in a different time. Replete with moments of foreshadowing, in which the present is latent with future events that happen in the past (such as Marty's 'well history is gonna change', and Lorraine's 'if grandpa hadn't hit him, then none of you would have been born'), *Back to the Future* seems to be ideal territory in which to manipulate cinema's normal time-sense. The film, however, undertakes a vigorous assertion of the time-sense of classical cinema. In one contemporary, *Highlander*, the point of view is repeatedly moved between distant historical periods through a number of graphic techniques (e.g. the camera moves upwards towards the dark ceiling of Madison Square Garden's underground car park, penetrates it and emerges out of the ground in sixteenth-century Glenfinnan), all of which signal the audience to acknowledge a resetting of the film's temporal register. By contrast, as Richard Maltby points out, *Back to the Future*

remains firmly, inevitably, in the present. However much the plot may disrupt the space–time continuum within its fiction (a time paradox, explains Doc, in the second film, 'could cause a chain reaction that would unravel the very fabric of the space–time continuum and destroy the entire universe'), the audience progresses through a narration staged in its own continuous present tense, moving from beginning to end according to its internal, tightly organized, dramatic logic.[111]

There is just one exception. When Marty returns to the present, we stay with Doc as he cheers and looks up towards the clock tower. This is followed by a shot of the clock tower, the two shots comprising a shot pattern known as an eyeline match. But then a police helicopter enters the shot from behind the clock tower. This edit forces the audience to revise the common assumption that editing patterns maintain the same time and space, and so, momentarily, to become more conscious of the habits that are always working to make the comprehension of film possible.

Back to the Future, however, does also confront the time-sense of classical cinema in one major respect. In addition to the two options listed above – a) flashback, and b) the rare shift into the past tense – we ought to add c) a shift into the future tense. According to the theory of multiple parallel realities that is laid out in the 1989 sequel, at the end of the first film Marty is living in the wrong reality. The ending, for example, ranks number one on cracked.com's list of six most depressing happy endings in movies for precisely this reason. 'How long until they push to have Marty institutionalized, since every memory from his childhood is from some bizarre ultimate reality that no one else shares?'[112] Yet this altered 1985 is acceptable for the overwhelming majority of viewers. This is, in part, because the changes are small compared with those that the film prompted the viewer to envision, and because of the singularly American intensity of the ideal of individual instrumentality. But it is also a direct product of cinema's time-sense. Although 1985 is presented as the narrative's 'present' (it is not technically the historical present, as the date given is the 25–26 October 1985, slightly in the future of both the production and the release dates), both 1985 and 1955 confront the viewer as discrete presents. Because the unfolding present of *Back to the Future* is set in 1955 for the majority (63 per cent) of the film's narrative duration, the viewer implicitly identifies 1955 as the story's present. Consequently, the film's closing view of the changed 1985 confronts the viewer as the future of the time that, for 69 per cent of the film thus far, film's temporal aspect has worked to establish as the present. So rather than a different present from the one that opened the film, the new 1985 is the logical projected future of the film's real present, and consequently matches perfectly the circumstances of the 1955 that Marty has just left. This also serves to make the threat of incest less potent; the situation where Lorraine is Marty's guardian is in the future of the film's acquired present.

In this sense, cinema (although not, as some have claimed, the film camera) is equivalent to a time machine, and not because it allows one vicarious time travel, but because it endorses one of the majority components of theories of time travel.[113] In January 1887, long before the summer–autumn of 1894 when he wrote the work published as *The Time Machine*, H. G. Wells first encountered the postulate in geometry that our reality might be four-dimensional. Resisting the majority view that this fourth dimension was a further spatial dimension that humans were merely incapable of perceiving, Wells derived the notion that this hypothetical fourth dimension was time, and, by early 1888, was drafting his first time-machine story, serialised as 'The Chronic Argonauts' from April to June. In 1891, still reworking these ideas for wider publication, Wells wrote, but did not publish, a factual article entitled 'The Universe Rigid', which hasn't survived. Remnants of this material in *The Time Machine* suggest that, in this lost article, he had argued that if time is a dimension, and if it is only different from the other three in that we tend to move slowly along it without intending to, then it is theoretically possible, with a temporal technology equivalent to such spatial assistance as a balloon, to move along that axis more freely, and in more than one direction. If this is the case, then the 'present' is merely the point on the time axis that the consciousness of any given observer intersects, making for an infinity of presents instead of the traditional forward-moving single 'now'. Travelling 7,926 years forwards on that axis, one would experience a different present, rather than the future of a privileged 'present' 7,926 years earlier. This means that the universe is a four-dimensional given, in which all of time has already happened – hence the title of the article.[114] Most of the time-travel narratives since Wells have followed this idea. Stephen King's 'The Langoliers' (1990), where travelling into the past means pausing in an uninhabited, energy-less world while the present moves onwards, is the only exception of which we are aware.

The major attribute that *Back to the Future* attains from employing time travel is a slightly fantastical reliance on exposition for narration. Richard Maltby remarks that in *Back to the Future Part II*, Zemeckis and Gale introduced such complex plotlines that they were forced to include a lecture by Doc on the cause and effect of old Biff's journey to 1955.[115] Although the sequel's influential explanation of 'branching universe' theory was not anticipated by the first film, the complexity of cause and effect nonetheless necessitates monologue that in other dramatic circumstances would be superfluous, in particular Marty's exteriorised thought processes when alone in the DeLorean. Where a character would ordinarily be shown working out their options and intention through eyeline matches with relevant objects, Marty just has to say, 'Damn it Doc, why did you have to tear up that letter? If only I had more time! Wait a minute. I got all the time I want. I got a time machine. I can just go back early and warn him.' The fantastical aspect of time travel is thus accompanied by a treatment of character removed from the normally light-handed narration of realist cinema. Another example is the hyperbole of the film's narrative process. Although time-travel films do not necessarily require knowledge of precisely *when* the present is (as *mise en scène* can clearly demonstrate when the destination time stands in relation to the present), *Back to the Future* is based on the conceit of a rather short journey into the past. Consequently, the presentness of the present receives narrative emphasis from the outset, a statement of the month and year featuring just 73 seconds after the film's narrative time commences, in the radio advertisement for Toyotas.

Although the film's account of 1955 and 1985 may derive from a post-modern spatialisation of time, the film itself does not participate in this spatialisation of time. Indeed, for a time-travel film, *Back to the Future* revels in showing the pure passing of time. (By contrast, Francis Ford Coppola's *Peggy Sue Got Married* [1986], an alternative treatment of many of the same elements of plot and humour, pays no particular attention to the normal passing of time.) This is evident even at the opening. Following the Universal logo, the screen becomes black, and then the words 'Steven Spielberg presents' appear, initially implying that, as with the logo, story time has still not yet commenced, but then the sound of a ticking clock fades up, indicating that time is passing in the story space (and that it probably started passing as soon as the black screen appeared), and another thirteen seconds of ticking elapses, while 'A Robert Zemeckis film' and then 'Back to the Future' are shown, before visuals appear. Ticking, a pure signifier of time passing, revises images that do not necessarily connote the passing of story time into temporal units. Zemeckis and Gale also emphasised the normal passing of time when they had Doc Brown explain that 'At exactly 1.21 a.m. and zero seconds we shall catch up with Einstein and the time machine'. They also chose to stage their race-against-time climax around a big index of the passing of time: the tower clock. The two deadlines enact the passing of time by showing paired scenes of dramatic action moving towards the same single moment.

This attention to the normal passing of time is linked to cinema's implicit success in emulating the temporal dimension of human experience. *Back to the Future* even presses this advantage, stretching film's implicit impression of a continuous present to its limits. For example, it is common for a film's version of events to take less time than the events themselves. The point of view is merely

elliptically moving, usually via edits, over moments of 'dead' time. Cinema usually signals this by showing changes in circumstances: a change from night to day, a change in a character's location or a clock showing one time fading into the same clock at a later time. In the opening scene of *Back to the Future*, although no such overt signal of the passing of time occurs, the editing is also elliptical. Marty comes in when the clocks are showing 7.53 a.m. and the clocks go off when they show 8 a.m., yet only 4 minutes and 40 seconds of screen time has elapsed. In this common method of relating to story time, cinema draws on literary conventions because it does not intrinsically contradict them, as this does not substantially alter the principle, inherent in emulating the human experience of time, of a forward-moving present. For the account of events to last longer than the events themselves, however, is extremely uncommon in film. Although literary conventions exist that allow a description of an event to take more time to read than the event described would take to occur, film by and large possesses no equivalent, because its basic function of emulating an experience of time cannot allow for the instantaneous backward jumps necessary for an account of an event to last longer than the event itself. During the clock-tower scene, these principles are put to good use. As the clock moves from 10.00 to 10.04, varying amounts of time elapse between each movement of the minute hand. Minute 10.00 to 10.01 is narrated in just 36 seconds of film time, while minute 10.03 to 10.04 is covered in just 46 seconds. This is a normal ratio of the passing of time in the story space to the passing of filmic time, even in the most dramatic of situations. By contrast, minutes 10.01 to 10.02 and 10.02 to 10.03 take up 1 minute 47 seconds and 1 minute 46 seconds of screen time respectively. Zemeckis had to fit a lot of actions and events from two locations into these two minutes. Yet very few viewers will perceive that these two story minutes actually take 3 minutes and 37 seconds to show, or that they are being shown sequentially events that actually happen simultaneously (e.g. Marty punching the car and Doc reaching for the cable). In the absence of an overt prompt to indicate that the point of view has moved back in time to describe an event occurring at the same time as an event already shown, audiences assume that time is moving forwards.

If *Back to the Future* is nostalgic for earlier cinema, then this nostalgia is for a more concretely temporal cinema. This also suggests that while Sobchack sees cinema as one of the post-modern visual phenomena 'spatialising' time, then this might be a mistaken interpretation of cinema's innate tendency also to temporalise time.

Conclusion: 'Your kids are gonna love it'

Hey Rick, it's your cousin Marvin! Marvin Astley!? You know that
mediocre generic sound you've been looking for? Well listen to this!
'Meet the Quagmires', *Family Guy*, Season 5, Episode 18 (20 May 2007)

Kurt! Kurt! It's your cousin. Your cousin Marvin Cobain!? You know
that new sound you're looking for? Well listen to this!
'That 90s Show', *The Simpsons*, Season 19, Episode 11 (27 January 2008)

The climactic scene of the 24 February 1981 first draft of *Back
to the Future* goes like this. Having fixed Marty's future, he and
Brown ('Professor Brown' in this draft) travel to Nevada, where (as
Marty learned in the 1980s), the army is carrying out what will be its
last surface nuclear tests. Brown smuggles him past the perimeter
fence of a nuclear test site with the then-immobile time machine in
the back of a truck, the projecting area of its 'Time Beam' now
conveniently encompassed by a fridge that Brown has lined with lead.

Marvin Astley

Brown parks the truck in the fake town that the army have constructed to test the effects of the blast, and leaves via motorbike with a mannequin wearing Marty's jacket in the sidecar. Speaking with Marty from a safe distance via walkie-talkie, he instructs him to add the Coca-Cola that (as Marty accidentally discovered in the 1980s) fuels the time machine's power converter, but Marty realises that it is in his jacket. Panicked, Brown tells Marty to abandon the plan, get inside the fridge and hope that the lead lining will save him from the nuclear explosion. Instead Marty runs to a nearby house, in which mannequins watch *Howdy Doody*, and which are so realistic that their fridges are fully stocked, finds some bottles of Coke, uses them to power the time machine, and then has to race against time to get the truck into the right place so that when the bomb explodes, the radiation striking it will be at the correct level, while also avoiding the attentions of the artillery unit that has spotted him.

Twenty-seven years later, the second scene of Steven Spielberg's *Indiana Jones and the Kingdom of the Crystal Skull* (2008), set in 1957: Indy escapes from his captors at 'Hangar 51', and treks across the Nevada landscape until he comes across an isolated town. Laundry lines are full, sprinklers water the gardens and a television plays the *Howdy Doody* show, but he soon finds that the town is inhabited only by mannequins. An air-raid siren and warning announcement draw his attention to a nearby hill, where a cartoonish nuclear bomb sits in a scaffold about to be detonated. Indy scrambles fruitlessly for a place to shelter as the announcement counts down, and then frantically turfs out the contents of a fully stocked fridge before clambering inside, the dolly-in showing a plaque that reads 'lead lined' just before Indy shuts the door with seconds to spare. The detonation turns the town into an inferno and then blasts it to splinters, spitting a conspicuous fridge out beyond the blast radius, the fridge rolling to a halt and disgorging Indy. Dr Jones then adds a mushroom cloud to the list of spectacular surroundings against which he has been silhouetted.

Having offered to produce *Back to the Future* in 1981 when it was in this form, and to do so when nobody else would, Spielberg had reason to remember Zemeckis and Gale's ultimately unused climax, and he and Lucas would certainly have discussed this borrowing with their old acquaintances in planning *Crystal Skull*. The race against time in the surface nuclear test site, the encounter with the town creepily inhabited by mannequins and the hypothetical possibility of surviving a nuclear explosion by sheltering in a fridge all seem to have appeared to Spielberg as such appealing cinematic units that, although they were unfeasible in 1984–5, could still be usefully employed almost a generation later. On top of the many and widespread resonances of *Back to the Future* in popular culture – including Marvin Astley and Marvin Cobain – its film-making priorities are still current. New New Hollywood, although now even more reflexive (witness the fade from the Paramount mountain to the molehill at the beginning of *Crystal Skull*, an allusion to the fade from Paramount mountain to story-space mountain at the beginning of *Raiders of the Lost Ark*), continues, at the time of publication, to thrive.

Notes

1 Bob Gale and Robert Zemeckis, interview with Lauren Puthero, *Back to the Future Trilogy*, DVD, Universal, 2002, disc 1.

2 David Colker and Jack Virrel, 'The New New Hollywood', *Take One*, vol. 6 no. 10 (September 1978), pp. 19–23.

3 Thomas Elsaesser was one of the first to describe this new form of Hollywood, in 'The Pathos of Failure. American Films in the 1970s: Notes on the Unmotivated Hero', *Monogram*, vol. 6 (1975), pp. 13–19.

4 Jon Lewis, *Whom God Wishes to Destroy: Francis Coppola and the New Hollywood* (Durham, NC: Duke University Press, 1995), p. 143. Thomas Elsaesser, 'The New New Hollywood: Cinema beyond Distance and Proximity', in Ib Bondebjerg (ed.), *Moving Images, Culture and the Mind* (Luton: University of Luton Press, 2000), pp. 187–204. Elsaesser, 'American Auteur Cinema: The Last – or First – Picture Show?', in Alexander Horwath, Thomas Elsaesser and Noel King (eds), *The Last Great American Picture Show: New Hollywood Cinema in the 1970s* (Amsterdam: Amsterdam University Press, 2004), pp. 37–70, 55. David Bordwell, *The Way Hollywood Tells It: Story and Style in Modern Movies* (London: University of California Press, 2006), p. 25.

5 See, for example, Thomas Schatz, 'The New Hollywood', in Jim Collins, Hilary Radner and Ava Preacher-Collins (eds), *Film Theory Goes to the Movies* (London: Routledge, 1993), pp. 8–36; Jim Hillier, *The New Hollywood* (London: Studio Vista, 1992); Bordwell, *The Way Hollywood Tells It*, pp. 1–4.

6 Noël Carroll remarks that after the flopping of *Star!*, the success of *Easy Rider* the following year convinced the debt-ridden major studios to abandon genre projects and back more such experimental products, including *Alice's Restaurant* (dir. Arthur Penn, 1969), *Zabriskie Point* (dir. Michelangelo Antonioni, 1970), *Drive, He Said* (dir. Jack Nicholson, 1971), *Brewster McCloud* (dir. Robert Altman, 1970), *Harold and Maude* (dir. Hal Ashby, 1971), *Mean Streets* (dir. Martin Scorsese, 1971), *Five Easy Pieces* (dir. Bob Rafelson, 1970), *M*A*S*H* (dir. Robert Altman, 1970) and *Carnal Knowledge* (dir. Mike Nichols, 1971). Noël Carroll, 'Back to Basics', *Wilson Quarterly*, vol. 10 no. 3 (Summer 1986), pp. 58–69, 63.

7 New New Hollywood did not mean an industrial return to old Hollywood, however, as the major distributors all financed low-cost independent productions – which would have been impossible during the studio era – in addition to their blockbusters and sleeper-hit-potential star vehicles.

8 Robert Zemeckis and Alan Silvestri, quoted in 'The Making of Back to the Future', 1985, *Back to the Future Trilogy*, disc 1.

9 Estimate based on United States of America, *Statistical Abstract of the United States, 1979* (Washington, DC: US Bureau of the Census, 1980); *Motion Picture Association of America US Economic Review*, 1998, p. 24.

10 Robert Zemeckis, interview, *Academy of Achievement*, 29 June 1996, accessed 20 February 2009, <www.achievement. org/autodoc/page/zem0int-1>, para. 12.

11 Spielberg remarked on the importance of late-night film viewings on television in an interview in 1979. Bill Davidson, 'Will 1941 Make Spielberg a Billion Dollar Baby?', *New York Times*, 9 December 1979.

12 Gale and Zemeckis, interview with Lauren Puthero.

13 Vivian Sobchack, *Screening Space: The American Science Fiction Film* (New York: Ungar, 1987), p. 274.

14 Gale and Zemeckis, interview with Lauren Puthero.

15 Quoted in Tom Shone, *Blockbuster* (London: Simon & Schuster, 2004), p. 123.

16 Carroll, 'Back to Basics', pp. 58–69, 65.

17 Gale and Zemeckis, interview with Lauren Puthero.

18 Zemeckis and Silvestri, quoted in 'The Making of Back to the Future'.

19 Stephen Prince, 'Movies and the 1980s', in Stephen Prince (ed.), *American Cinema of the 1980s* (Oxford: Berg, 2007), pp. 1–21, 10.

20 Peter Krämer, *The New Hollywood: From* Bonnie and Clyde *to* Star Wars (London: Wallflower, 2005), p. 116.

21 Spielberg's biographer remarks that, as a producer, 'Spielberg has regarded himself largely as the filmmakers' advocate, protecting them against studio interference.' Joseph McBride, *Steven Spielberg: A Biography* (London: Faber & Faber, 1997), p. 384.

22 Gale and Zemeckis, interview with Lauren Puthero.

23 Timothy Corrigan, *A Cinema without Walls* (London: Routledge, 1991), p. 42.

24 Peter Krämer, ' "Want to Take a Ride?": Reflections on the Blockbuster Experience in *Contact* (1997)', in Julian Stringer (ed.), *Movie Blockbusters* (London: Routledge, 2003), pp. 128–40, 132.

25 Kristin Thompson, *Storytelling in the New Hollywood: Understanding Classical Narrative Technique* (London: Harvard University Press, 1999), pp. 77–102.

26 Bordwell, *The Way Hollywood Tells It*, p. 122.

27 Quoted in 'The Making of Back to the Future'.

28 Timothy Shary, *Teen Movies: American Youth on Screen* (London: Wallflower, 2005), p. 75; Stephen Prince, *Movies and Meaning*, 3rd edition (London: Pearson, 2004), p. 425; Andrew Gordon, '*Back to the Future*: Oedipus as Time Traveller' (1987), in Sean Redmond (ed.), *Liquid Metal: The Science Fiction Film Reader* (London: Wallflower, 2004), pp. 116–25, 118; Sobchack, *Screening Space*, p. 276.

29 Gordon, '*Back to the Future*: Oedipus as Time Traveller', p. 122.

30 Gale and Zemeckis, interview with Lauren Puthero.

31 Michael Allen, *Contemporary US Cinema* (London: Longman, 2003), p. 193.

32 Geoff King, *New Hollywood Cinema* (London: I. B. Tauris, 2002), p. 137.

33 Stephen Prince, *A New Pot of Gold: Hollywood under the Electronic Rainbow, 1980–1989* (Berkeley: University of California Press, 1999), p. 288.

34 Shone, *Blockbuster*, p. 124.

35 These common types are described by Geoff King and Tanya Krzywinska, *Science Fiction Cinema* (London: Wallflower, 2000), p. 43.

36 King, *New Hollywood Cinema*, p. 52; James Chapman, *Cinemas of the World:*

Film and Society from 1895 to the Present (London: Reaktion, 2003), p. 142; Krämer, *The New Hollywood*, p. 97. Bordwell, *The Way Hollywood Tells It*, p. 53.

37 Steve Neale, 'Hollywood Corner', *Framework*, vol. 19 (1982), pp. 37–9, 37.

38 Carroll, 'Back to Basics', p. 58.

39 Andrew Britton, 'Blissing Out: The Politics of Reaganite Entertainment', *Movie*, vol. 31 no. 2 (Winter 1986), pp. 1–42, 5.

40 Norman Kagan, *The Cinema of Robert Zemeckis* (London: Taylor Trade, 2003), p. 220; Sobchack, *Screening Space*, p. 250.

41 Ina Rae Hark, ' "Daddy, Where's the FBI Warning?" Constructing the Video Spectator', in Matthew Tinkcom and Amy Villarejo (eds), *Keyframes: Popular Cinema and Cultural Studies* (London: Routledge, 2001), p. 74.

42 Carroll, 'Back to Basics', p. 69.

43 Bordwell, *The Way Hollywood Tells It*, *passim*.

44 Gale and Zemeckis, interview with Lauren Puthero.

45 In Pal's film, the opening montage shows clocks floating in abstract space and fades their various ticking sounds in and out. During the first scene, in which the time traveller's waiting dinner guests discuss his lateness, they are shocked by the simultaneous chiming of the large number of clocks mounted on the surrounding walls.

46 Quoted in 'The Making of Back to the Future'.

47 Thomas Doherty, *Teenagers & Teenpics: The Juvenilization of American Movies in the 1950s* (Boston: Unwin Hyman, 1988), p. 3.

48 Shary, *Teen Movies*, p. 18.

49 Doherty, *Teenagers & Teenpics*, p. 75.

50 Ibid., p. 80.

51 Shary, *Teen Movies*, p. 54.

52 Ibid.

53 Jon Lewis, *The Road to Romance and Ruin: Teen Films and Youth Culture* (New York: Routledge, 1992), p. 119.

54 Jonathan Bernstein, *Pretty in Pink: The Golden Age of Teenage of Movies* (New York: St Martin's Griffin), p. 138.

55 Lewis, *Road to Romance and Ruin*, p. 3.

56 John Belton, *American Cinema/American Culture* (Columbus, OH: McGraw-Hill, 2005), pp. 322–5.

57 Mark Winokur, ' "Passing" as a Strategy', in Lester Friedman (ed.), *Unspeakable Images* (Chicago: University of Illinois Press, 1991), p. 202.

58 Robert Miklitsch, *Roll over Adorno: Critical Theory, Popular Culture, Audiovisual Media* (Albany: State University of New York Press, 2006), p. 128.

59 Winokur, ' "Passing" as a Strategy', p. 202.

60 Hernán Vera and Andrew Gordon, *Screen Saviors: Hollywood Fictions of Whiteness* (Oxford: Rowman & Littlefield, 2003), p. 125.

61 Steve Bailey and James Hay, 'Cinema and the Premises of Youth: "Teen Films" and Their Sites in the 1980s and 1990s', in Steve Neale (ed.), *Genre and Contemporary Hollywood* (London: BFI, 2002), p. 218.

62 Ibid., p. 219.

63 Ibid., p. 233.

64 Prince, *A New Pot of Gold*, p. 218.

65 Vivian Sobchack, 'Cities on the Edge of Time: The Urban Science Fiction Film', in Redmond (ed.), *Liquid Metal*, p. 222.

66 Susan Faludi, *Backlash: The Undeclared War against Women* (London: Chatto & Windus, 1992), p. 1.
67 Ibid., p. 17.
68 Ibid., p. 74.
69 Marsha Kinder, 'Back to the Future in the 80s with Fathers & Sons, Supermen & Peewees, Gorillas & Toons', *Film Quarterly*, vol. 42 no. 4 (Summer 1989), pp. 2–11, 5.
70 Gale and Zemeckis, interview with Lauren Puthero.
71 Ibid.
72 Robin Wood, *Hollywood: From Vietnam to Reagan* (New York: Columbia University Press, 1986), p. 172.
73 Richard Maltby, *Hollywood Cinema: An Introduction* (Oxford: Blackwell, 1995), p. 321.
74 Kinder, 'Back to the Future in the 80s', p. 4.
75 Ibid., p. 5.
76 Robert Zemeckis, interview with Charlie Rose, *Charlie Rose*, 13 October 1994, Rose Communications Inc.
77 This is a kind of inversion of the aesthetic that can be observed in *Ghostbusters*, which contains a 1950s ambulance that has been retrofitted with all kinds of antennas and unknowable modern-day technological gizmos.
78 Gale and Zemeckis, interview with Lauren Puthero.
79 Britton, 'Blissing Out', pp. 1–42.
80 Ibid., p. 15.
81 Wood, *Hollywood: From Vietnam to Reagan*, pp. 168–9.
82 Ibid.
83 Julian Borger, 'Nuclear Weapons: How Many Are There in 2009 and Who Has Them?', *Guardian Datablog*, 7 September 2009 (<www.guardian.co.uk/news/datablog/2009/sep/06/nuclear-weapons-world-us-north-korea-russia-iran#data>).
84 This macabre sense of 'fun' regarding the nuclear, embodied in part by Doc Brown's fearless excitement over his project, resonates with a similar attitude in the works of the American nuclear strategist Herman Kahn (1922–83), who, in his public persona, theorised the previously unthinkable outcomes of nuclear war with gleeful optimism and a focus upon the possibilities of survival. An account of Kahn that focuses upon this unique mode of engaging with the nuclear can be found in Sharon Ghamari-Tabrizi's *The Worlds of Herman Kahn: The Intuitive Science of Thermonuclear War* (Cambridge, MA: Harvard University Press, 2005).
85 Joseph M. Siracusa, *Nuclear Weapons* (Oxford: Oxford University Press, 2008), p. 63.
86 Robert J. McMahon, *The Cold War* (Oxford: Oxford University Press, 2003), p. 61.
87 Quoted in 'The Making of Back to the Future'.
88 Dean Baker, *The United States Since 1980* (New York: Cambridge University Press, 2007), p. 105.
89 Constance Penley, 'Time Travel, Primal Scene and the Critical Dystopia' in Annette Kuhn (ed.), *Alien Zone: Cultural Theory and Contemporary Science Fiction* (London: Verso, 1990), pp. 116–27, 117.
90 Gale and Zemeckis, interview with Lauren Puthero.

91 Andrew Gordon lists further instances of this motif. See 'Back to the Future: Oedipus as Time Traveller', p. 119.

92 Wyn Wachhorst, 'Time-Travel Romance on Film: Archetypes and Structures', Extrapolations, vol. 25 (1984), pp. 340–59, 340.

93 Ronald Reagan, State of the Union Address, 4 February 1986, in Brad Borevitz, State of the Union, accessed 14 March 2009 (<stateoftheunion. onetwothree.net/texts/19860204. html>).

94 Wachhorst, 'Time-Travel Romance on Film', p. 350.

95 Vivian Sobchack, 'Postfuturism', in Redmond (ed.), Liquid Metal, pp. 220–7, 220.

96 Ibid.

97 Quoted in 'The Making of Back to the Future'.

98 Sobchack, Screening Space, p. 274.

99 Robert Zemeckis, quoted in 'Making the Trilogy: Chapter 1', Back to the Future Trilogy, disc 1. In the February 1981 draft of Back to the Future, Doc (then Professor) Brown even launches into a monologue on how time can be seen as a dimension, which, although he is cut off by Marty's swift exit, is redolent of The Time Traveller's explanation, to his dinner guests, of the nature of temporal geometry at the beginning of The Time Machine. Marty even serves as The Time Traveller's missing sidekick. Whereas The Time Traveller comments to his auditors that he sorely missed the use of a Kodak when he was in the year 802,701 (H. G. Wells, The Time Machine:

An Invention, 1895 [London: Penguin, 2005], p. 54), Doc, who has forgotten his video camera, can call on Marty to fetch it for him, and when it is taken on the time journey, it provides vital information ('1.21 gigawatts!') that enables Marty to return from 1955.

100 Quoted in 'The Making of Back to the Future'.

101 J. Hafele and R. Keating, 'Around the World Atomic Clocks: Predicted Relativistic Time Gains', Science, vol. 177 no. 4044 (14 July 1972), pp. 166–8.

102 See, for example, Jack Kroll, 'Having the Time of His Life', Newsweek, 8 July 1985, p. 76.

103 J. Hoberman, 'Spielbergism and Its Discontents', Village Voice, 9 July 1985, p. 45.

104 Gordon, 'Back to the Future: Oedipus as Time Traveller', p. 119. Constance Penley is among those to categorise Back to the Future in this way (Penley, 'Time Travel', p. 120).

105 Gordon, 'Back to the Future: Oedipus as Time Traveller', p. 121.

106 Jay Ruud, 'Back to the Future as Quintessential Comedy', Literature/Film Quarterly, vol. 19 no. 2 (1991), pp. 127–33.

107 Andrew Gordon, 'You'll Never Get Out of Bedford Falls!: The Inescapable Family in American Science Fiction and Fantasy Films', Journal of Popular Film and Television, vol. 20 no. 2 (Summer 1992), pp. 2–8, 7.

108 Ibid., p. 3.

109 Ibid.

110 This epigraph is by Carl Sagan: 'Physicists propose that two alternate histories, two equally valid realities, could exist side by side: the one you

know, and the one in which you don't exist. Time itself may have many potential dimensions, despite the fact that we are condemned to experience only one of them' (Carl Sagan, *Cosmos* [New York: Random House, 1980], p. 173). Instead of explaining that Marty had created a second 1985 that left the first 1985 extant but inaccessible, they preferred instead to treat time as a single narrative that can be changed. Zemeckis and Gale have provided a list of answers to frequently asked questions about the trilogy, including explanations of the time-travel plotlines in the two sequels. (Robert Zemeckis and Bob Gale, Frequently Asked Questions, BTTF.com, nd, accessed 16 March 2009 [<www.bttf.com/film_faq.htm>]).
111 Maltby, *Hollywood Cinema*, p. 309.

112 Colm Prunty and Rick Kay, 'Six Most Depressing Happy Endings in Movies', cracked.com, nd, accessed 2 March 2009 (<www.cracked.com/article_16570_p2.html>).
113 Constance Penley, for example, claims that 'cinema has the properties of a time machine' (Penley, 'Time Travel', p. 119), and Malta Hagener remarks that '[f]ilm itself is a time machine' (Malta Hagener, 'Back to the Future', in Jürgen Müller (ed.), *Movies of the '80s* [London: Taschen, 2002], p. 331), while Marina Warner calls the film camera 'the first time machine of modernity' (Marina Warner, Introduction, *The Time Machine: An Invention*, by H. G. Wells [London: Penguin, 2002], p. xiii).
114 Wells, *The Time Machine*, pp. 4–5.
115 Maltby, *Hollywood Cinema*, p. 309.

Credits

Back to the Future
USA/1985

Directed by
Robert Zemeckis
Produced by
Bob Gale
Neil Canton
Written by
Robert Zemeckis
& Bob Gale
Director of Photography
Dean Cundey
Edited by
Arthur Schmidt
Harry Keramidas
Production Designed by
Lawrence G. Paull
Music by
Alan Silvestri

©1985. Universal City
Studios, Inc.
Production Companies
Steven Spielberg
presents
a Robert Zemeckis film
[opening logo] Universal
– an MCA company
[end logo] Amblin
Entertainment

Executive Producers
Steven Spielberg
Frank Marshall
Kathleen Kennedy
**Unit Production
Managers**
Dennis E. Jones
Jack Grossberg

**Production
Co-ordinator**
Maureen Osborne-Beall
**Assistant Production
Coordinator**
Rob Stevens
Production Associates
Steven Talmy
Diana L. Hayes
Anthony Gibson
Jeffrey R. Coates
Location Manager
Paul Pav
Production Controller
Bonnie Radford
Production Accountant
Leanne Moore
Assistant Accountants
Lynn D. Ezelle
Robert R. Draney
Ann Furia
**Assistant to Mr
Zemeckis**
Gail Oliver
Assistant to Mr Canton
Babette T. Gorman
Assistant to Mr Gale
Eileen Omaye
**Assistant to Mr
Spielberg**
Julie Moskowitz
**Assistant to Mr
Marshall**
Mary T. Radford
**Assistant to Ms
Kennedy**
Kate Barker
Assistant to Mr Repola
Judy Thomason

**Post-production
Supervisor**
Arthur Repola
2nd Unit Director
Frank Marshall
1st Assistant Director
David McGiffert
2nd Assistant Director
Pamela Eilerson
**2nd Unit 1st Assistant
Director**
Mitchell Bock
DGA Trainee
Concetta Rinaldo
Script Continuity
Nancy B. Hansen
Casting by
Mike Fenton
Jane Feinberg
Judy Taylor
**2nd Unit Director of
Photography**
Raymond Stella
Camera Operator
Raymond Stella
1st Assistant Camera
Clyde E. Bryan
2nd Assistant Camera
Stephen Tate
Still Photographer
Ralph Nelson
**Chief Lighting
Technician**
Mark D. Walthour
**Assistant Chief
Lighting Technicians**
Thom Marshall
Michael Paul Orefice

Electrical Lighting Technicians
George LaFountaine
Steven R. Mathis
Anthony Wong
Key Grip
Ronald T. Woodward
Best Boy Grip
Dan Cooper
Dolly Grips
Dick Babin
'Wild' Will MacLean
Grips
Michael Salts
Chuck Schray
Dic Alexander
Visual Effects Produced at
Industrial Light & Magic
(Marin County, California)
Special Effects Supervisor
Kevin Pike
Special Effects Foremen
Neil Smith
David Wischnack
Special Effects
Steve Suits
Kimberley Pike
Sam Adams
Richard Chronister
William Klinger
Assistant Film Editors
Peter N. Lonsdale
Barbara Dixon
Apprentice Film Editors
Roger Jaep
Charles Simmons
Art Director
Todd Hallowell

Set Decorator
Hal Gausman
Lead Person
Art Smedley
Production Illustrators
Andrew Probert
Dick Lasley
Set Designers
Joseph E. Hubbard
Marjorie Stone McShirley
Cameron Birnie
Property Master
John Zemansky
Assistant Property Masters
'Dangerous' Bob Widin
Joe Pfaltzgraf
Construction Coordinator
Ernie Depew
Paint Foreman
Kirk D. Hansen
Standby Painter
Jim Passanante
Scenic and Graphic Artist
Al Gaynor
DeLorean Time-travel Consultant
Ron Cobb
DeLorean Construction Coordinator
Michael Scheffe
Costume Designer
Deborah L. Scott
Key Costumer
Julie Starr Dresner
Men's Costume Supervisor
Brian Callahan

Make-up Created by
Ken Chase
Hairstylist
Dorothy Byrne
Title Design
Nina Saxon
Colour Timer
Terry Haggar
Opticals by
Movie Magic
Negative Cutter
Donah J. Bassett
Music Supervisor
Bones Howe
Music Editor
Kenneth Karman
Assistant Music Editor
Deborah Zimmerman
Music Software
Dick Bernstein
Music Scoring Mixer
Dennis Sands
Orchestrations
James Campbell
Soundtrack
'The Power of Love' written by Huey Lewis, Chris Hayes, performed by Huey Lewis and the News; 'Back in Time' written by Huey Lewis, Chris Hayes, performed by Huey Lewis and the News; 'Heaven Is One Step Away' [written and] performed by Eric Clapton, produced by Phil Collins; 'Time Bomb Town' [written and] produced by Lindsey Buckingham, Richard

Dashut, performed by Lindsey Buckingham; 'Mr Sandman' [written by Pat Ballard], performed by Four Aces; 'The Ballad of Davy Crockett' [music by George Bruns, lyrics by Tom W. Blackburn], performed by Fess Parker; 'The Wallflower (Dance with Me Henry)' [written by Johnny Otis, Hank Ballard, Etta James], produced by Maxwell Davis, performed by Etta James; 'Night Train' produced by Bones Howe, performed by Marvin Berry and the Starlighters; 'Pledging My Love' [written by Ferdinand Washington, Don D. Robey], performed by Johnny Ace; 'Earth Angel (Will You Be Mine)' [written by Curtis Williams, Jesse Belvin, Gaynel Hodge], produced by Bones Howe, performed by Marvin Berry and the Starlighters; 'Johnny B. Goode' [written by Chuck Berry], produced by Bones Howe, performed by Marty McFly [Mark Campbell] with the Starlighters

Original Soundtrack available on
MCA Records and Cassettes
Choreographer
Brad Jeffries
Production Sound Mixer
William B. Kaplan
Boom Operator
Earl F. Sampson
Utility Sound
Darcy Vebber
Re-recording Mixers
Bill Varney
Tenny Sebastian II
Robert Thirlwell
Dan Leahy
Supervising Sound Editors
Charles L. Campbell
Robert Rutledge
Sound Editors
Larry Carow
Sam Crutcher
Janice Hampton
Scott Hecker
John A. Larsen
Harry B. Miller III
Chuck Neely
Bruce Richardson
Fred Stafford
Jerry Stanford
Assistant Sound Editor
Larry Fallick
Apprentice Sound Editor
Sonny Pettijohn
Processed Sound Effects
Craig Harris

Foley by
John Roesch
Supervising ADR Editor
Larry Singer
ADR Editor
Alan Nineberg
Assistant ADR Editors
Rod Rogers
Glenn T. Morgan
Stunt Coordinator
Walter Scott
Stunts
Richard E. Butler
Charlie Croughwell
Loren Janes
Max Kleven
Bernie Pock
Spiro Razatos
Robert Schmelzer
John-Clay Scott
Per Welinder
Bob Yerkes
Animal Handlers
Robert Weatherwax
Richard Caulkins
Transportation Manager
Gene Schwartz
Transportation Coordinator
John Feinblatt
Transportation Captain
Bob R. Cornell
Transportation Captain/Picture Cars
Tom Garris
Craft Service
Ramon B. Pahoyo
Unit Publicist
Marsha Robertson

Special Thanks to
Mark Campbell
Tim May
Stephen Semel
Gregg Landaker
Steve Maslow
Ron Hitchcock
Photographic Illustration
Company (Burbank,
California)
Group IV Scoring Facility
TV Extracts
The Honeymooners (CBS
Inc./Viacom)

CAST
Michael J. Fox
Marty McFly
Christopher Lloyd
Dr Emmett Brown
Lea Thompson
Lorraine Baines
Crispin Glover
George McFly
Thomas F. Wilson
Biff Tannen
Claudia Wells
Jennifer Parker
Marc McClure
Dave McFly
Wendie Jo Sperber
Linda McFly
George DiCenzo
Sam Baines
James Tolkan
Mr Strickland
Jeffrey Jay Cohen
Skinhead
Casey Siemaszko
3-D

Billy Zane
Match
Harry Waters Jr
Marvin Berry
Donald Fullilove
Goldie Wilson
Lisa Freeman
Babs
Cristen Kauffman
Betty
Elsa Raven
clock-tower lady
Will Hare
Pa Peabody
Ivy Bethune
Ma Peabody
Frances Lee McCain
Stella Baines
Jason Marin
Sherman Peabody
Katherine Britton
Peabody daughter
Jason Hervey
Milton Baines
Maia Brewton
Sally Baines
Courtney Gains
Dixon
Richard L. Duran
terrorist
Jeff O'Haco
terrorist van driver
Johnny Green
scooter kid #1
Jamie Abbott
scooter kid #2
Norman Alden
Lou
Read Morgan
cop

Sachi Parker
bystander #1
Robert Krantz
bystander #2
Gary Riley
guy #1
Karen Petrasek
girl #1
[George] Buck Flower
bum
Tommy Thomas
**Granville 'Danny'
Young**
David Harold Brown
Lloyd L. Tolbert
Starlighters
Paul Hanson
Lee Brownfield
Robert DeLapp
Pinheads

uncredited
Huey Lewis
high-school band
audition judge

Dolby Stereo
Colour by
Technicolor
Panaflex Camera and
Lenses by
Panavision
1.85:1
Released in both 35mm
and 70mm (blow-up)
prints
MPAA no.
27831
IATSE

Released in the US by Universal Pictures on 3 July 1985, MPAA rating PG, at circa 117 minutes. Released in the UK by UIP on 4 December 1985, BBFC certificate PG (no cuts), at 115 minutes 51 seconds/10,427 ft +10 frames.

Filmed from 26 November 1984 to 20 April 1985 on location in South Pasadena, City of Industry, Chino and Newhall (all in California), and at Universal Studios (Universal City, California, USA). Budget reported as $19 million.

Credits compiled by Julian Grainger

Don't miss out! Sign up to receive news about BFI Film and TV Classics and win a free bundle of books worth £100!

ach book in the BFI Film and TV Classics series
nours a landmark of world cinema and television.

With new titles publishing every year, the series
present some of the best writing on film and TV
available in print today.

In order to enter, first sign up via:
http://www.palgrave.com/resources/mailing.asp
and then simply email bfi@palgrave.com with your
e, email address and NEW BFI CONTACT in the subject header.

offer ends: 05/01/11. The winner will be contacted via email by 31/01/11.